D1806381

A PRACTICAL GUIDE
TO
REPAIR AND MAINTENANCE
OF HOUSES

by
Peter Mytton-Davies

International Thomson Business Publishing
London NW3 3TP

2

Published 1988

© International Thomson Business Publishing

ISBN

A 'Building Trades Journal' Book

Typeset by Quickset, 184/186 Old Street, London EC1
Printed and bound in Great Britain
by The Grange Press,
Butts Road, Southwick, Sussex

Contents

Introduction

In nearly every centre of population we see many sub-standard houses in which people are still living. Unfortunately there are enough of these to refute any suggestion that the nation's housing stocks are now adequate. The slowing down of house building means that it is now more important than ever for us, as a nation, to put our dwellings into good repair and maintain them to a reasonably high standard. Consequently the subjects of repair and maintenance discussed in this book are of supreme importance to those who live — or who want to live — in houses. While it is socially desirable for the house building programme to press forward, it is equally important that our existing housing stocks should be brought up to an acceptable standard and, once having been repaired, should be maintained in reasonable condition. This alone should be sufficient argument in favour of spending time, effort and money on repairing houses worth keeping and then maintaining them at an acceptable standard. But there is also another powerful argument in favour of spending money on repairs. Every year house prices seem to rise, especially in the South East. As the value of such houses increases, so it becomes even more important to retain existing housing stocks in good condition. Many run down houses could be made, not only habitable, but also pleasant places in which to live, if repaired properly and maintained adequately.

This goal is one which local authorities sometimes find difficult to achieve in their public sector programmes. Building new housing estates may be costly, but there is more to show for the money. However repairs cost less than new estates and safeguard existing housing stocks. Perhaps the private house owner has even stronger reason to remember this since, in his or her case, the asset is personal property. When properly maintained the value of such an asset is likely to increase year by year while the repair which is needed this year is likely to be more difficult and costly next year. Some builders prefer working for local authorities which they regard as good credit risks. Other builders, usually the smaller ones, prefer to concentrate on the private sector for building houses and for the repair and maintenance market.

Keeping a house in a proper state of repair and making sure that it is maintained in accordance with a high standard are twin responsibilities which no house owner can afford to neglect. For most people house purchase is the most important financial transaction they undertake throughout their lives and their houses become their most valuable assets.

For many the business of acquiring a house involves several different costs, especially if they are 'first time buyers'. First there is the cost of house hunting. Not only does this involve travelling expenses of one kind or another, it also takes time. For folk with a living to earn time often equals money. Then there is the purchase of the house itself, and the legal charges. On top of these costs there is the expense of moving in and of setting up home. Even if some of the many items needed to turn a house into a home are given to a newly married couple, the cost of setting up a home can be considerable. However there is one cost which is, perhaps, the most frightening of all and which tends to be overlooked by many because it is more or less hidden. Many house buyers have to borrow at least part of the money for buying their property. Of these many do not take into account the cost of the mortgage interest.

All these costs have to be considered to arrive at the true cost of home ownership. Even those fortunate buyers with ready cash to buy should remember that, by devoting capital to that end, they are reducing the total amount that they will have to invest elsewhere.

Repairing and maintaining older houses

Repairing older houses often poses special problems requiring careful study if satisfactory solutions are to be found. Such work may need the professional approach of the archeologist, the penetrating eye of the surveyor, the expertise and the discriminative flair of the architect, the scientific knowledge of the technologist, the skill and experience of the builder and a helpful attitude on the part of the builder's merchant who may be asked to supply unusual building components and materials for which there is generally little demand.

To put run down houses into a satisfactory state of repair the enthusiasm for the project on the part of the council's building inspector and the attitude of the planning authority to the proper maintenance of period property, is likely to be important. This is particularly the case when the proposed work also includes structural alterations or additions requiring byelaw and planning permission as well as routine maintenance.

If the proposed work is extensive whoever is paying for it will require a deep pocket or, failing that, an obliging bank manager or far sighted building society. If there is a mortgage which is not discharged the lender should be informed if the work goes beyond routine repair and maintenance and, particularly if structural alterations are contemplated; the same goes for the ground landlord if the property is leasehold. If material alterations or additions are planned these parties should be informed even if money to pay for them does not have to be borrowed. The insurance company carrying the risk on the building should also be told.

Listed property

Some older houses are listed as historic buildings. For these the Secretary of State for the Environment is responsible for compiling lists of buildings of special architectural or historical interest. These lists form the basis of national and local conservation policies and are kept under constant review.

The principles governing the selection of buildings to be listed were originally hammered out by an expert committee consisting of architects, antiquaries and historians and these principles are still followed. Every building built before 1700 which is still more or less in its original condition is listed. So are many built between 1700 and 1840 but houses built during this period have to be selected before being listed. Between 1840 and 1914 buildings have to be of definite quality and character to qualify for being listed; these are selected to reflect the work of the most eminent architects of the period. Eventually some buildings built between 1914 and 1939 will be listed; a start on this listing has already been made.

To show their relative importance the listed buildings are classified in three grades. At present only about 2 per cent of all listed buildings fall into grade 1 which embraces buildings of exceptional interest. Grade 2 is subdivided into two parts, Grade 2 and Grade 2*. Ordinary grade 2 buildings consist of houses and other structures of special interest which warrant every effort being made to preserve them. Some particularly important buildings which come into grade 2 category are designated grade 2*. As a category grade 3 is now no longer commonly used. It applied to buildings which, while not qualifying for the statutory list, were considered nevertheless, to be important. Today many of these buildings are now judged to be of special interest by current standards, particularly in cases where they possess group value. These are bring added to the statutory lists as these are revised.

When deciding which buildings are to be listed particular attention is given to four points:
(1) The value of buildings of certain types for either architectural or planning reasons or from the point of view of illustrating social and economic history.
(2) Technological innovation or virtuosity such as, for example, the early use of prefabrication, cast iron or concrete.
(3) Houses or other buildings associated with famous historical characters or events.
(4) The value of a building as part of a group such as, for example, an early effort at town planning. Certain squares, terraces and model villages come into this category.

At one time the Department of the Environment issued two lists. One of these was a provisional list containing detailed descriptions of buildings and their grades; the other was a statutory list containing the addresses of the buildings. The Department's Inspectorate of Historic Buildings is, at the time of writing, resurveying various local authority areas. The reports of these inspectors are forming the basis for producing revised statutory lists in a new form. Details of grading and descriptive notes are now being included in one cumulative statutory list for each local authority area. The buildings listed in the statutory list are legally subject to the provisions of the scheme. The statutory lists are available for inspection at the National Monuments Record, Fortress House, 23 Saville Row, London W1X 2HE or at the office of the relevant county or district council. While listed buildings may not necessarily be preserved intact in all circumstances they must not be demolished unless the case has been fully examined and permission for the demolition to go ahead granted. If alterations are necessary a similar examination must be undertaken before permission is granted and the alterations made must preserve the character of the building as far as possible. The 'Listed Building Consent' required before such work can begin must be obtained from the local planning authority, the district borough council or the Secretary of State. Details of the application procedure can be obtained from the planning department of the appropriate body. To demolish or alter a listed building without official consent is an offence carrying a penalty which is unlimited or up to 12 months' imprisonment or both.

To be allowed to redevelop a site occupied by a listed building both listed building consent for the demolition and planning permission for the new building will be required. Planning permission alone does not authorise the demolition of the listed building.

If proposed alterations to a listed building are sufficient to affect its character and the proposed alteration amounts to development for which planning permission is required (as distinct from a general permission authorised by the General Development Order), the express authorisation of both planning permission as well as listed building consent is necessary. A refusal to give listed building consent or the granting of such consent subject to conditions not acceptable to the applicant may produce an appeal to the Secretary of State. This usually results in a local public enquiry being held. The appeal procedure is the same as the procedure for appeals against a refusal to grant planning permission.

The Royal Commission on Historic Monuments must be given an opportunity to make records of any building for which listed building consent for its demolition has been given. Owners of such buildings who want to demolish them should tell this Commission at Fortress House, 23 Saville Row, London W1X 2HE either before or immediately after consent to demolish a listed building is obtained. The local planning authority should be able to provide a form for this purpose. Before starting the demolition work the Royal Commission must be given at least a month or more during which time the Commission's representatives must be allowed access to the building and given an opportunity to make any records they require. This period runs from one of two dates: the date when listed building consent is given or the date on which the Royal Commission is notified, whichever is the later. If the Royal Commission completes its work during the month or states that it does not propose to make records of it, demolition may then begin. In case the regulations change, check before taking action.

Repairs to listed buildings

The owner of a listed building is required to take reasonable steps to preserve it. Should the owner fail to do this the local authority may be entitled to buy it compulsorily with the consent of the Secretary of State. If the building is unoccupied the local authority may be entitled to repair it and recover the cost from the owner. If the owner deliberately neglects the building in order to redevelop the site, in addition to acquiring the building the local authority may do so at a price which excludes the value of the site for redevelopment.

In certain circumstances grants or loans from central government funds or from local authorities may be available to help owners of listed buildings needing repair and maintenance. This help is at the discretion of the body providing it. The fact that a house or other building is listed does not carry automatic entitlement to a grant. However there are also exchequer grants, for the Secretary of State has the authority to make grants for the repair or maintenance of buildings of exceptional architectural or historic interest. Such buildings have to be really outstanding and only a few qualify. Consequently the scope of these grants for such listed buildings is limited. In this matter the Secretary of State is advised on the making of grants by the Historic Building Council for England; enquiries should be addressed to the Secretary of the Council at the Department of the Environment, 25 Saville Row, London W1X 2BT.

In contrast to the above, local authorities have wider scope concerning the making of grants. They make grants for any building or architectural or historical interest. These grants are not confined to outstanding buildings or even to buildings which are listed. Such grants may be made by the London borough councils and by county and district councils. It is appropriate to address enquiries about such grants to the local authority concerned. In some cases it may be possible to get a house improvement grant for a listed building which is to become a dwelling. The statutes which are apposite to listed buildings and possible grants for them include the following: Historic Buildings and Ancient Monuments Act 1953; Local Authority (Historic Buildings) Act 1962; Town and Country Planning Act 1971; Town and Country Planning (Amendment) Act 1972; Town and

Country (Amenities) Act 1972; Local Government, Planning and Land Act 1980.

The observations made above relate to listed buildings but, quite apart from grants or loans for these, there are grants which may be available for houses which are not listed buildings and which, in many cases, have virtually no particular architectural or historic value.

Grants

A system of grants designed to provide some measure of financial help where dwellings are not up to a reasonable standard and need money spending on them, has been in operation for some years. Such grants may be helpful, especially to owner-occupiers of properties with modest rateable values. In some cases a grant may be mandatory; other grants may be discretionary. It is essential for application for a grant to be made to the appropriate authority before any work is started. Without an opportunity for the local authority to consider the work proposed and to approve or amend the proposal, the applicant will not be eligible for a grant.

Since local authorities tend to have rather different administrative management structures, the first step is to locate the grant-awarding department and discuss the project with the appropriate officer. It is also important to appreciate that the percentage of the total cost of the proposed work which qualifies for a grant may vary from time to time and place to place. Grants which depend on the rateable value of the property concerned may also vary between one authority and another. There are likely to be ceilings above which grants will not be awarded. Obviously the difference between the amount of the grant and the cost of the work has to be found. The applicant who does not find it convenient to pay immediately should approach a bank or building society or any other reputable source of finance.

Although this book is concerned mainly with the repair and maintenance of houses, it may be helpful to mention a few details about grants administered by local authorities. In general the reader should appreciate that the idea behind the awarding of grants is to improve sub-standard property with inadequate facilities rather than to contribute towards the cost of maintenance.

The mandatory grant which cannot be refused if the application meets all the statutory requirements is designed to help meet the cost of equipping a dwelling with standard amenities such as a toilet in the house, flat or bungalow, a bath (or shower), kitchen sink, wash hand basin and running hot and cold water. This is called an intermediate grant.

Apart from the mandatory grant mentioned above there are discretionary grants which the local authority may decide to give or not to give. One of these is the improvement grant. This type of grant may be made for a variety of proposed projects designed to improve a house, to help convert a large house into flats and, in some cases, for repairs. The house or flat must have been built before 1961. Here are five possible improvements which may qualify for some measure of financial help by a grant; inserting a damp proof course; rewiring or installing electricity power points; repointing brickwork if the wall needs such treatment; removing a fireplace or chimney breast; making the front door watertight.

In some circumstances an improvement grant may help towards the cost of the work which certainly needs to be done but which could prove too expensive for the owner to pay for without some financial help. In the case of houses which need structural repairs a repair grant may be available for those built before 1919. This type of grant is only given, if it is given, when substantial structural repair is needed and where the property concerned is worth repairing. Repairs to roofs, walls, foundations and floors might qualify but ordinary routine maintenance would not. In England and Wales special grants may sometimes be made towards the cost of standard amenities and for providing the means of escape from fire for houses shared by more than one family. Again the reader is reminded that these are discretionary grants and cannot be claimed by applicants 'as of right'. Moreover, if they are awarded, they will only cover part of the total cost, the rest of which will have to be found.

In designated general improvement areas and housing action areas grant aid may be more favourable. In some places and in certain circumstances a grant may be available for loft installation and lagging water pipes and tanks where such work has not already been done. It may also be possible to get some help if people in the house are disabled or handicapped. A leaflet prepared by the Department of the Environment entitled 'Home Improvement Grants' should be available at public libraries or from the Citizens Advice Bureax.

In addition to whatever financial help which grant aid may provide there is a great deal of advice and information to be had providing you hunt for it.

Information sources for the building trades and public
Appendix II lists names, addresses and telephone numbers of various sources of information which may be useful to readers. The following brief notes about some of these bodies may be helpful to readers with houses to look after, especially period houses since these, being relatively old, usually need repairing when ownership of them changes hands. Older houses also tend to need maintenance more frequently. Victorian houses and those built this century before the start of the Second World War, are often solidly built and benefit from a more generous use of timber and some other materials than some houses built more recently. Nevertheless such Victorian houses may be in need of repair and maintenance and a good deal of the text of this book is primarily devoted to their care.

Modern houses, which are often on either the brick and block system or the timber frame construction tend to develop rather different faults if they prove in some degree to be less than fully satisfactory. So part of this book will be devoted to the repair and maintenance of houses which have been built since the Second World War. With these points in mind, let us take a brief look at some of the bodies mentioned in Appendix II. Because Appendix II gives the postal addresses and telephone numbers of the corporate bodies, this information is not listed here.

The Brick Development Association represents the great majority of the leading brick manufacturers in the UK. In its efforts to promote the best possible use of bricks the BDA provides a wealth of information and technical data about its member's products. A great deal of this information is presented in such a way that it will be readily appreciated and understood by members of the public; the more advanced literature is addressed to a technical audience such as architects, civil engineers, surveyors, planners, specifiers and, of course, builders, especially bricklayers.

The British Standards Institution is the national standard making organisation. Quality assurance is the basis of the BSI's work which includes operating the kitemark and the Safety Mark Schemes. The Registered Firm Scheme assesses the ability of a company to manufacture to a system in line with BS 5750, a 6 part British Standard which deals with various aspects of British Standards.

In this country the British Board of Agrement is the officially recognized body for testing building materials and components and issuing certificates. Building products awarded the certificate are respected by builders 'merchants' and the building industry generally.

The Building Centre in London provides a permanent exhibition showing a wide selection of building materials, components and service. There is a wealth of manufacturers' literature on a wide range of products available to the public; in addition to this a great deal of technical information is available to the building industry. Thus the data available from the Building Centre's information services can be helpful to both the public and the trade. The public utilities such as gas and water have useful representation as do bodies such as the National Coal Board. There are also building centres in Bristol, Manchester and Glasgow.

The Building Conservation Trust is an independent educational charity which operates a permanent exhibition concerned with house maintenance and home improvements. The exhibition explains techniques, the use of materials and components and is housed on three floors of an apartment in Hampton Court Palace. A charge is made for admission.

The Building Research Advisory Service and the Building Research Establishment (Department of the Environment) provide vital sources of information for the building and construction industries. Research is undertaken into many aspects of building and construction techniques including those for combating damp and mould. The Fire Research Station's Field Investigation carries out interesting studies into fire, and smoke-spread in buildings and domestic fire deaths. At the establishment's laboratories at Princes Risborough matters such as reducing the cost of maintenance for window joinery and the comparative cost and performance standards of other building materials may become subjects for research and analysis. The Advisory Service disseminates technical information discovered by such studies and is helpful to both the public and the building industry.

The Cement and Concrete Association offers users of these products a service of technical information and advice, based on the findings of research stations. Information is also collected on a world wide basis.

The Association's training centre provides courses on concrete practice and technology. The design of concrete buildings also receives attention.

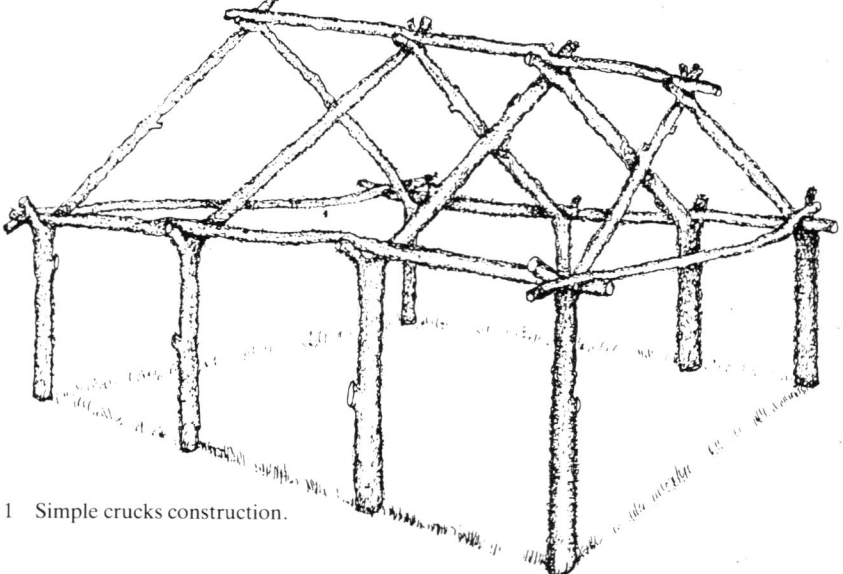

1 Simple crucks construction.

Soon after being formed in 1957 the Civic Trust pioneered new techniques of land reclamation and the planting of trees on derelict land. Since then the trust has worked, sometimes under difficulties, to achieve its objectives to conserve the best of the past and to encourage high standards for the future. The Civic Trust Awards have played a leading role in raising the standards of new development. For example, the Lee Valley Regional Park master plan was first devised by the Civic Trust. The trust's influence and hard work in Wirksworth has resulted in a revival of this small town in

Derbyshire. The Heritage Education Group has been the means of encouraging many young people to take an active interest in their surroundings. While the trust's activities have been concerned with districts and buildings, there has also been considerable interest in houses, their preservation and development. Films for which the trust has been responsible include 'A Future for the Past', 'Look Stranger' and — on video — 'The Civic Trust Scrapbook'.

The Historic Building and Monuments Commission of English Heritage, which is perhaps more widely known by its unofficial but shorter title of 'English Heritage' is a body which should interest readers concerned with the repair and maintenance of old buildings and houses. A good deal of useful and interesting information is available from this source.

The National House Building Council which produces an excellent publication 'Home Owner's Handbook' (and which sets out to provide ten years structural insurance cover for new homes built by its Registered Builders), is a highly informative booklet dealing with many aspects of the business of buying a house likely to interest readers of this volume, whether they be house purchasers or builders. The publication mentioned gives detailed advice to the house buyer and outlines the two rather different systems of building domestic property, brick and block and timber-frame. Services such as water, central heating, electricity and gas are also discussed and there is some useful advice on saving energy. Under the general heading of 'Taking care of your new home' there are useful hints on maintenance.

Other sections deal with the legal rights of house buying, home security and hints for the handyman in his new home. There is also a useful index.

The Timber Research and Development Association is an independent research body devoted to ensuring the best and most economical use of timber especially in the construction and building industries. The association's principal laboratories are equipped with mechanical and fire testing facilities.

WARM was formed in 1979 to co-ordinate the promotion of wood and solid fuel appliances which are either manufactured in this country or imported. Information relating to wood burning and appliances for use with such fuel is available.

The Building Act 1984
From a legal point of view the Building Regulations for England and Wales made in accordance with the provisions of the Building Act 1984, represent considerable changes when compared with the framework of the regulations previously in force. There have been important procedural changes, the new regulations being drawn up, largely in the form of performance standards. These performance requirements are, to a great

extent, to be observed in conjunction with explanatory Approved Documents. In time procedures for approval may include, as one of the possible options, approval by certain professionals such as architects. However this has not yet been decided.

The Building Act has, at the time of writing, been in force sufficiently long for some of its requirements to have been repealed already. Some of these relate to refuse and putting up buildings on sites contaminated by offensive waste matter. The provisions of the Act which have already been repealed have necessitated some alterations being made in the Building Regulations. It seems reasonable to suppose that the need for further amendments may arise from time to time. Without doubt readers — especially architects and builders — will welcome guidance and perhaps clarification of the current Building Regulations from such work as John Stephenson's book 'Building Regulations 1985 in Detail' revised. These words are being written before his latest book is published, but it may safely be assumed that the volume currently in preparation will be as useful as that author's previous work on the subject.

The role of builders' merchants

This introduction has discussed various corporate bodies and the grants system which may be helpful to readers; directly helpful to readers who are householders and indirectly helpful to readers who are builders since grants may stimulate their customers to have work done. There has also been some mention of legislation relating to building and the Building Regulations. However, so far there has been no mention of the important role played by the builders' merchants. Such merchants not only sell goods, but they also act as unofficial, unpaid advisors in many cases. This role for the builders' merchant is increasing as the demarcation line between this trade and that of the d-i-y superstore or shop becomes ever more blurred.

The builders' merchants play a vital part in the whole business of repairing houses and maintaining them in good repair, whether they sell to builders or to d-i-y enthusiasts. Consequently it is entirely appropriate that this book and others in the same series, should be available along with everything else in builders' merchants as well as in d-i-y outlets. The experienced builders' merchant usually has very sound advice to offer his customers when it comes to choosing between one brand of material or component and another. It is to be hoped that, in addition to helping builders and d-i-y enthusiasts, by selling this series of books which aim to be practical guides on different aspects of building, there will be a solid advantage to merchants as well. Whatever benefits householders by showing them how to repair and maintain their property and whatever benefits builders by providing them with technical information, will also benefit the merchants. A large proportion of their turnover comes from the need to repair and carry out routine maintenance of houses. The merchants, like the builders, benefit from the desire of the public to live in houses which are kept in repair and well maintained.

Chapter 1
A GENERAL LOOK ROUND THE SUBJECT

During the early thirties house building represented a depressed industry. The market for new and existing houses was sluggish and, with a few minor ups and downs, remained sluggish throughout the decade. The advent of World War 2 necessitated major movements of the population. Most of the South Coast and parts of the East Coast were evacuated. Children were taken out of London and other high risk places to the relative safety of the country or, in some cases, to other countries such as, for example, Canada.

The air raids on London and many other major cities wrought havoc with Britain's housing stock and, indeed, with other types of building as well as domestic dwellings. When the war ended the building industry — or what the war had left of it — faced daunting problems. There were shortages of workers, of materials, of available capital. Priority had to be given to building projects considered essential and urgent in the national interest. While the restrictions which this imposed may well have been justified and necessary, they did not help builders to set about the task of replacing domestic property destroyed by enemy action. Controls on building materials lasted several years.

Before the war many architects had been much concerned with the repair and maintenance of houses. But the years following the war produced a new set of conditions and, consequently a new economic and cultural environment in which the architects had to work.

As the years went by new building materials and methods began to be introduced. Houses of modest size were produced in factories and erected speedily on sites. These 'Prefabs' were designed to last thirty years; some remained in service longer; many became shabby before their intended life span. 'Prefabrication' became a magic word in the world of building.

Factory-made houses offered — or appeared to offer — a solution to the problem of housing large numbers of people quickly. In time land became harder to find and more expensive to buy. Methods of prefabrication were still used but the term began increasingly to refer to modules for high rise blocks. The architects began to link hands with the structural engineers; some of the merchant banks and local authorities put the capital together for the developers to undertake large scale housing projects.

The architects found a new technology at their disposal. In the area of domestic property they often had to think of housing estates rather than individual dwellings. Although various schemes were launched to repair and maintain existing housing stocks, it was professionally far more glamorous to design and be concerned with new houses. Also, a thriving market for the services of the British architect and the engineer was developing overseas. It was often far better business to design a giant complex for an oil-rich country than to bother about the restoration of a Georgian crescent. The repair and maintenance of houses, and especially of period houses, became the Cinderella of the building world.

Today the position is very different. While houses in some of the inner cities have fallen before the bulldozer, there is a growing interest in setting older houses in repair and maintaining them in the sort of condition which reflects favourably on their owners. Moreover the standards of people have risen and house prices have done likewise. Consequently there are many people, among them a fair sprinkling of first time-buyers, who can only afford relatively modest houses but who are determined to make these as comfortable as possible. In the meanwhile the architect and the engineer are finding increasingly that less capital is available for the major construction projects both in this country and overseas which have occupied so much of their attention during recent years.

In the present economic environment even some of the large consulting engineers in the forefront of the construction industry are paying increasing attention to construction and building services such as air conditioning and heating monitored by sophisticated methods of automatic control; better and more economical ways of using energy in building; advanced methods of fire and security precautions; internal and external communications in large buildings. Such elements of this market which remain available have to be shared with other professionals overseas. Consequently, in Britain there is now a tendency for professionals here to take a more active interest in whatever opportunities present themselves for the restoration of period property.

While much of the repair and maintenance work being done today results from the desire of house owners to put their run down houses into good order, there is also a good deal of work needed to repair and maintain modern houses. Consequently, to provide an overall review of the position in the UK the opening chapter of this book must outline both activities —

the repair and maintenance of period houses and houses built, in many cases, relatively few years ago. Without such an opening review this volume could hardly expect to be a practical guide to its designated subject.

Period houses — preliminary steps

Any book of this nature should start at the beginning of the repair and maintenance programme. If the work is extensive and virtually amounts to repairing the property so that it adds up to a major restoration, the beginning must take the form of a survey — more or less detailed — and the preparation of drawings. For a project involving a significant amount of work and therefore a significant amount of expense, the survey should be carried out by a qualified surveyor or architect. Preferably, such a professional should have had experience in dealing with domestic property of different periods, including houses, flats and bungalows which have been built only relatively few years as well as older houses.

The drawings resulting from the survey should be prepared either in the surveyor's office or by the architect's draughtsman. It is usual to show new work in red or to adopt some other device to distinguish whatever is proposed from existing work. While a great deal of work done in drawing offices today is computerized there remains a high percentage of work which is done by traditional methods by skilled draughtsmen. Repair and maintenance work is often undertaken by relatively small builders many of whom have their own drawing departments or who get work from local architects. Consequently there is a good deal of drawing for work which fits the subject of this book which is executed by hand in the traditional way. Not only is the drawing needed to show the builder's client what should be done, but it is also required as an instruction to the craftsmen and other workers on the building site.

The surveyor or architect will also need to retain a copy and if the proposed work has to be submitted to the planning or local authority to obtain planning and by law permission, a suitable number of copies will have to be made. In the case of proposals which it is hoped, will be granted aided, the authorities concerned will need plans and another set will be required if it is proposed to carry out work on a listed building for which special permission has to be obtained. Moreover sets of plans will be required if the owner of the house or his architect proposes to obtain estimates from different builders. For most domestic property and especially for jobs concerned with repair and maintenance contracts it is unusual to ask quality surveyors to prepare Bills of Quantities. However if a block of flats or a number of houses on a housing estate formed the basis of the job, it might be worth considering this step as perhaps the most efficient way of preparing the specification, tenders and estimates.

Many householders requiring repairs expect the builder to work on a fixed price contract basis. While it is understandable that householders should want to know their financial liability in advance it is often impossible for the jobbing builder to know what a job will cost before he has stripped away the building's outer fabric. Even with a professional survey some work may be needed to investigate the state of a period house before a firm price can be quoted.

The drawings needed will be a ground plan; a plan for each floor and the roof; front, side and rear elevations and various cross sections. If there are to be additional windows, the altering of a roof line or change in the means of access, a block plan showing the house or building under review in relation to the neighbouring properties may also be needed. But in many cases this will not be necessary if the job is only concerned with repair and maintenance. Should a block plan be required however, it is important that the points of the compass and the position of near-by buildings should be shown. So should the public highway.

Perpsective drawings are unlikely to be required, but if they are needed for some special reason they should be in isometric perspective. However sectional drawings (which depict a building as it would appear if sliced vertically into sections) can be useful if the proposed work extends beyond repair to the existing structure and includes some alteration to the internal layout. Very occasionally it might be worth preparing axonometric drawings of the interior of a house. Such a drawing would represent what a house would look like from above if it were possible to slice off the different storeys at ceiling level. The walls and internal doors would be shown.

Without doubt the householder should appreciate that the purpose of supplying drawings (usually in duplicate) to the local authority is to show exactly what the owner or agent acting for him/her has in mind. So the plans must be properly drawn up and to scale. Planning officers and building inspectors hate what they privately call 'pastry-board drawings' which fail to impart the necessary information. Such amateur efforts often have to be referred back to the self styled 'architect' for clarification. Unfortunately this often produces resentment on the part of the applicant who probably accuses the local or planning authority office of 'red tape'. But is it far better, from every point of view, for jobs which, by their nature and extent, require planning and by law-permission, to be sorted out in the early stages than for the applicant to have the work started only to have it disallowed at a later stage and then be required to change it. Fortunately many repair and maintenance jobs are unlikely to require planning and by-law permission unless a listed building is concerned or an application being made for grant aid.

What to look for in period houses
The chief enemies of period houses are damp, rot, insect and fungi attack, the ravages of polluted air and, especially in the case of timber-framed houses, mechanical failure of the structure due to some of the frames's

timbers becoming unable to resist the considerable stresses put on them any longer. Faulty foundations — if there are foundations — can also help to wreck an old structure especially after a prolonged dry, hot period when the site is a clay soil and sub soil. While these factors can make repairs necessary in old buildings of almost any age, there are failures which need attention which are particularly likely to occur in houses and other buildings built at certain historic periods.

Methods of construction developed and changed with each era and each form of construction was likely to develop its own particular faults in the fullness of time. The following brief notes may throw some light on the sort of faults which houses and other buildings of different periods may be expected to develop. Few readers are likely to live in mediaeval houses and those who do, are unlikely to lack advice — indeed, direction — from sources other than this book. Consequently, although the older the house perhaps the more likely it is to need repairing, only limited space will be devoted here to discussing very old domestic property. While many readers may live in comparatively old houses, or be builders carrying out repairs on such houses, the majority will be mainly concerned with houses built during Victorian times and onwards. So while there are brief observations on houses built before 1837 in this text most of this brief survey will be concerned with houses built more recently.

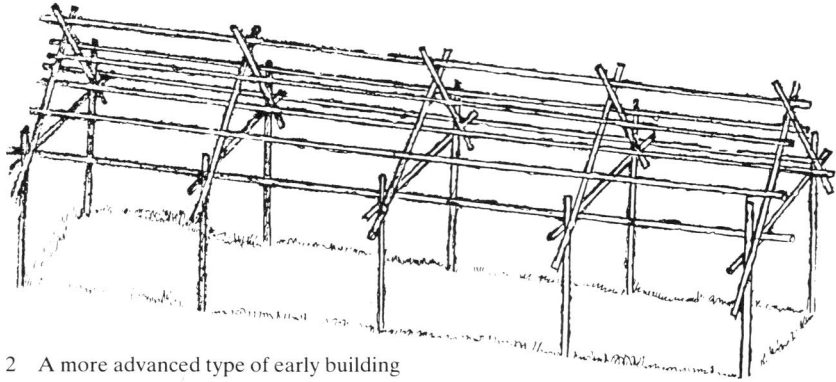

2   A more advanced type of early building

Most mediaeval buildings were four sided so that, considered on plan, they represented a rectangle. While this meant that they could be virtually as long as they liked when measured in the same direction as the ridge of the roof, their width was necessarily limited. Thatch, the popular roofing material for many old buildings, necessitated a steep pitch to allow water to run off. A steep pitch meant that the walls carrying the eaves had to be reasonably close to one another or the roof would be excessively high, thereby taking more timber and increasing the complexity of the builder's problems. Even when other roof coverings such as slate, tiles or riven stone were used the roof span remained an important consideration in mediaeval architecture. Churches, however, were given a feeling of width since they were designed on plan in the shape of a cross. Apart from increasing the floor space and accommodation within the building, the roof lines of churches thus became more interesting with their valleys and ridges. Hipped roofs also provided additional interest when employed on houses and other buildings.

The simple way to overcome the problem of having to make do with rather narrow buildings was to build two rectangular buildings side by side so that there were two gables at each end resembling an inverted w. These elevations were connected with side walls. Unfortunately while this form of construction permitted a squarish house to be built and was fairly common at a later date, in some parts of Britain — especially in the south east — it created a problem. A valley gutter had to run between the two gable roofs and this was liable to leak, to block with leaves and bird lime and to be inconvenient to clean. The two gable roofs side by side also meant that the central wall running through the house had to carry the weight of one side of each of the two roof constructions. However this was not necessarily too serious because the thrust of one roof on this wall was counter balanced by that of the other. However this form of construction came later, almost certainly because of the difficulty of creating a satisfactory valley gutter which would be leak proof. As late mediaeval buildings became bigger, i.e., longer the roof structures began to be divided into bays by means of *principal* trusses.

However the lean to was a popular feature in quite early domestic architecture. The effective width of the building could be increased by supporting the roof, not with walls, but with arches. This device, used with lean to extensions either side of the main building, formed the basis of a great deal of church architecture because it made it possible to have a wide bodied building instead of a relatively narrow one. The principle was later used in domestic architecture where it was put to use in various forms in some fine houses. By about 1600 the pitched roof was being widely used.

Roof pitches vary, of course, from one locality to another and, with more justification, between different materials. The following gives an indication of roof pitches for various roof covering materials:

Material	Angle with the horizon in degrees	Minimum Pitch
Thatch, tiles and shingles	45°	1/2
Single lap tiles	35°	1/35
Small slates	33°40°	1/3
Ordinary slates	26°34°	1/4
Large slates	21°48°	1/5
Lead, copper or zinc	3/4°	1/60
Asphalt	3/4°	1/60

It should be appreciated that for thatch the pitch given here is the minimum and some thatched roofs are set at 55° rather than 45°. Again the correct pitch for tiles varies somewhat with the design of the particular tile being used. The builder's merchant or the tile manufacturer will supply information for each kind. Thus the builder or even the d-i-y enthusiast should be able to obtain something suitable for the roof concerned when retiling is needed. The point should however be made that tiling a roof is a very big job for even the most enthusiastic do it yourselfer. Roof tiling is usually undertaken by specialists to whom many builders are content to hand over the job. If the experienced builder finds it best to use the services of the specialist, certainly the amateur should think long and deeply before deciding to attempt the job himself or (these days) herself. It should also be appreciated that some roofing materials such as asphalt which may be laid at a 1/60 pitch are used for what are termed 'flat' roofs.

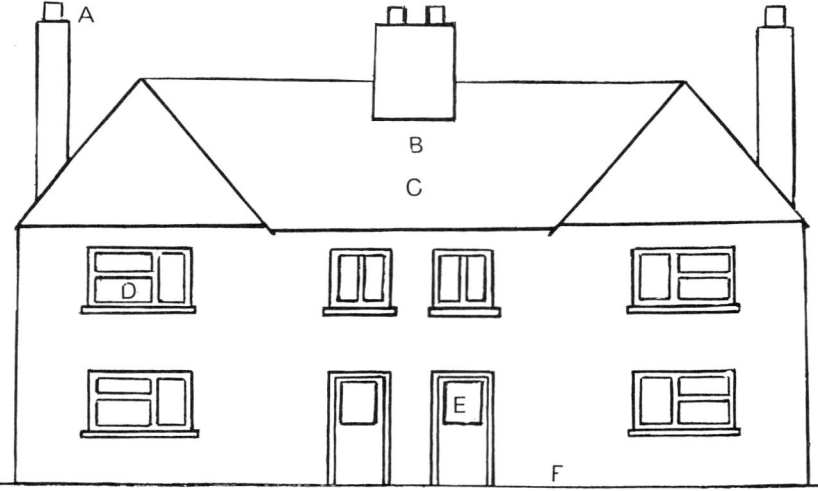

3   Points to look for in modern semi-detached houses.
A Is the chimney sound?
B Are there any flashings at the base of the chimney?
C Is the roof sound with all its tiles in place?
D Are the windows watertight?
E Do the doors fit properly?
F Is there a good damp proof course?

However to return to the early use of pitched roofs; before the end of the 16th Century the double unit of two rectangles side by side (on plan) had become reasonably well established, the builders (or perhaps the forerunners of the builders' merchants?) had found reasonable solutions to the problem of leak proof gutters. Also pitched roofs were being used more widely in both sacred and secular buildings. By 1600 many large houses were built with spine walls along the long axis and 17th Century architects became expert at designing great houses with roof spans which represented sound building practice and which could be constructed with timber locally available. Brick and stone were then becoming popular whereas, in mediaeval architecture, the builder's most commonly used materials were oak and, in many districts, wattle and daub as infill for the panels created by the oak.

Irrespective of the date of the building which is to be repaired and maintained, the architect or builder needs to have three types of drawing. These should be a plan of each floor, elevations showing what the outsides of the building look like and sections showing the system of construction being used and the height of internal features. Obviously such drawings cannot be made until a careful survey has been undertaken. If the house is very old its alignment may be awry and subsequent generations may well have altered the house from time to time. But without drawings to act as a guide the would-be repairer will have great difficulty in bringing a property back to something like its original state or, at least to a state in which it can be lived in with some degree of comfort. By the 17th Century the construction with its roof was termed a 'pile' while a wide roofed construction with a spine wall was called a 'double pile'.

The 17th Century also saw the squaring up of house plans and this resulted in hipped roofs. Thus the old gable ends of houses began to be questioned. Many considered that the gable end has had its day and that the way to build imposing looking houses was to have hipped roofs. Soon double-pile hipped roof with a wall plate all around the building became popular. During the 17th Century the spine wall remained in many cases, especially in the south east but, by the 18th Century, a couple of cross walls which passed across the building from front to rear began to be used.

Timber frame houses
A word should be said here regarding timber frame buildings. There are more such houses and cottages still about than might be thought possible because so many of them have had their timbers plastered over and hidden from view. So it is unlikely that a jobbing builder will go through his career without being asked to deal with such a house.

Until something like three hundred years ago timber was the universal building material in this country, except perhaps in Cornwall which had fewer trees and far more stone. In other places timber was often not replaced by stone until well into the seventeenth century. The Great Fire of London, for example did not take place until 1666 but it demonstrated the extent to which timber was employed in London's buildings. Manchester was also largely a "wooden city"; it was still full of timber buildings until well into the eighteenth century. During the seventeenth century it is

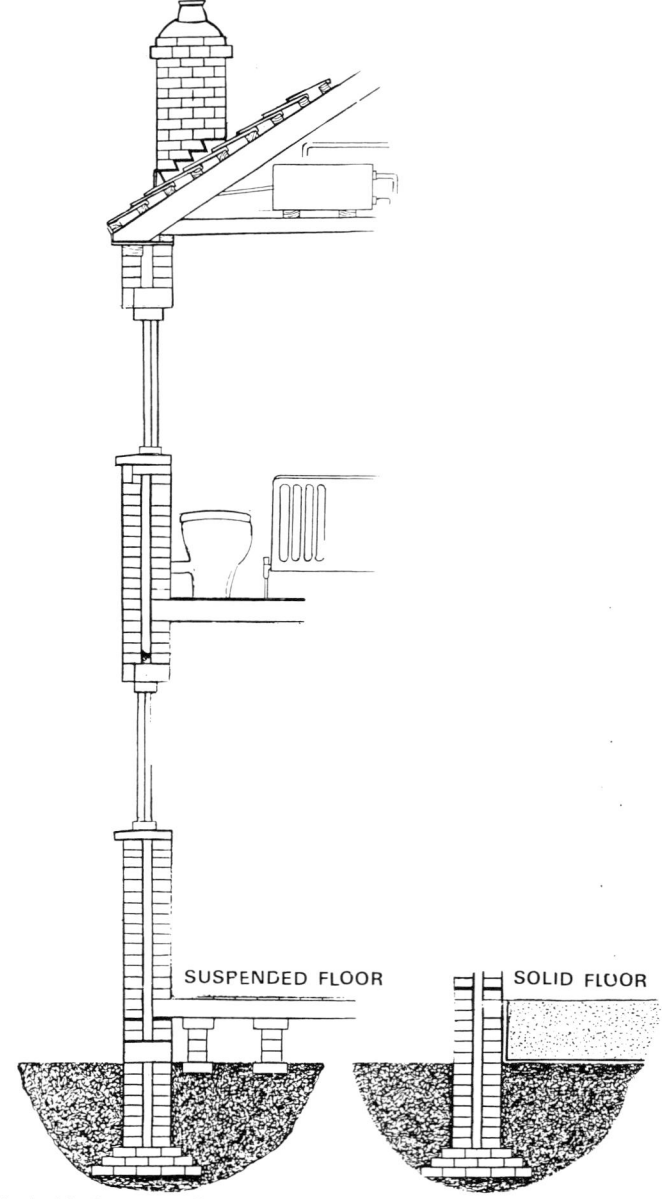

SUSPENDED FLOOR   SOLID FLOOR

4/5   Is the inside damp proof?
Look at this diagram. Is your hot water tank properly lagged and how about your cold supply?
Does the WC leak and do your radiators respond properly when they should? Are the
windows satisfactory? Is the dampcourse in good order? Have you a suspended floor or a solid
floor?

believed that there were some three million acres of forest land in the country.

Without doubt oak was the best timber available for building purposes. It was hard, strong and durable and it became harder with age. During the latter part of the sixteenth century it began to be used for quite humble cottages; previously it had mainly been reserved for finer and richer buildings. The best oak was that which had been grown on deep clay.

The sagging roof timber of oak which the modern builder may be called on to repair is likely to be due to the fact that little or no attempt was ever made to season the oak before it was used.

Indeed the large scantlings often needed made it impracticable to season such timber. Earlier oak had been plentiful and usually only the heart of the timber was used, the rest going for fuel. But as time went on builders started to economise on the size of their scantlings and these were reduced. Greater use was made of the rest of the tree. Some of the rafters still had their bark left on them.

The oaks were usually felled with a rather narrow axe although broad axes were sometimes used for very large trees. These were split into baulks with iron wedges and then cut to length with a two man saw. For the larger timbers such as the posts, bressummers and wall plates the baulks were shaped by the broad axe and then trimmed with an adze. Smaller timbers such as rafters, studs and floor boards had to be cut lengthwise with a two handed saw. This was done in a saw pit with two men — one working above the baulk and the other below. Morticed joints were formed with a chisel and mallet or sometimes with an auger which made holes, the rest of the wood being chopped out with a twibill. As far as possible this kind of work was carried out at ground level and then offered up.

Other forms of construction include both post and truss and also box frame. But before considering these let us take a brief look at what came to be known as cruck frame construction.

Cruck frame construction

With this method of building inclined timbers rose from the ground and met at the apex of the roof. Thus they served for walls and also as roof trusses. Usually the roof was thatched, the thatch extending down to the ground. There is some evidence to believe that cruck work was to be found only in the poorer types of cottage but this was confounded by the fact that, of the cruck work still standing today, the majority belong to a better class of property. Such houses occur in Wiltshire and Gloucestershire among other places.

The timbers for the cruck constructed houses were either straight or elbowed. many of the earlier examples had their timbers, known as "blades" made of the same tree trunk, this being split down the middle so that two posts with the same cruck in them could be used to make an arch.

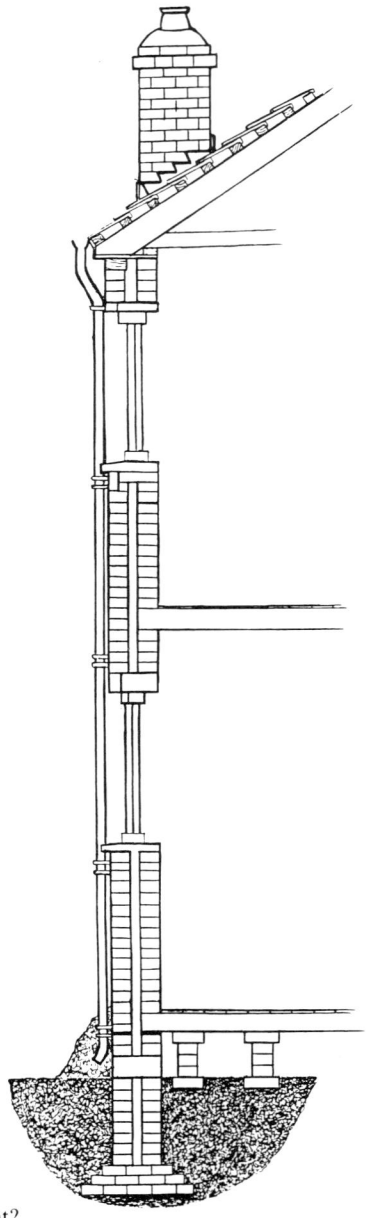

6   Is the outside watertight?
Look at this diagram. Points to observe include the chimney and its stack, the roof and the flashings, the guttering and the down pipes, the windows, the way the rafters are set into the wall, the way the ground floor is set up on pillars for air, the damp proof course and the foundations.

In some cases these arches, at each end of the building, were the only ones employed, but in others there was a series of arches, usually about sixteen feet apart. At first the blades were driven into the ground, but in later examples some kind of stone foundation was used.

It is unlikely that the average reader will be asked to repair a crucked framed cottage or house but this form of construction will be found if he or she is asked to do so. In the apex of the arches a lighter timber connected the rows. This was termed a ridgebeam. The ends or gables of such buildings were usually made with members of wood with infillings of mud reinforced with straw or hair. These tie beams or collars may occasionally need renewing in crucked houses. By the end of the fifteenth century this form of building was virtually abandoned except for the dwellings of the lower classes. Many such cottages were single storey, but there are examples of two storey cruck buildings.

Post and truss or box frame

It is more likely that the reader will be called upon to repair a cottage or house which is either built on the post and truss principle or is of box frame construction. Post and truss is sometimes called post and panel where it can be seen in the Midlands and North. Sometimes it is also found in the West. The weight of the roof is transferred to ground level by traverse frames spaced at intervals. Usually the posts are held together by a tie beam to which the principal rafters are fitted. About half way up the beams there are collars supported by a couple of vertical struts, one end being framed into the tie beam and the other into the collar. This forms what is called the tie beam truss. The purlins are let into the trusses and wall plates. These support the weight of the roof. They also support the common rafters whose function is to support the roof covering. To improve stability there may be diagonal braces between the vertical posts and wall plates. This means that the wall between the vertical posts is not structural; usually this has studs or light weight braces.

Box framed houses differ slightly from post and truss houses. Here the roof loads are taken on the external side walls, instead of having traverse frames. Such side walls offer a continuous bearing; they do not need any posts to divide the walls into bays. In this kind of construction the trusses or perlins are not necessary. Usually the roof pairs of rafters joined at the apex with collars are sufficient. Everyone has seen the box framed house which had vertical studs running up the height of each storey forming long panels. In contrast to this the post and truss construction which, with its far greater use of horizontal members, tends to form square shaped panels.

Close studding started to be popular in the latter part of the fifteenth century and remained in fashion until about the start of the seventeenth century. Both post and truss and also box frame have something in common. There is usually a plinth of stone, brick, flint or even oak which

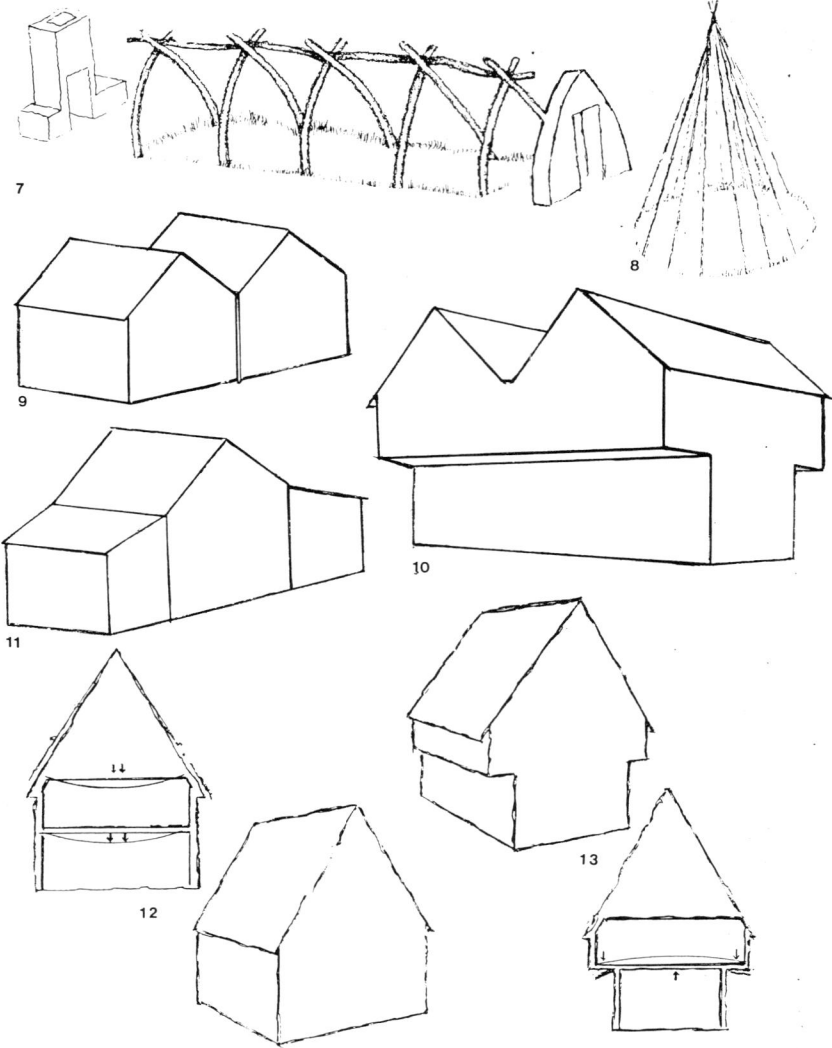

7   An old crucks building a suggestion of a fireplace at end a doorway at the other.
8   A very early building. It is doubtful if any of these are left today.
9   A double gable building — which increases the width.
10 A jettied building which incorporates sound principles.
11 Increasing the width of a building. This form of construction was often used in early churches.
12 Diagram showing the stresses of floor and ceiling.
13 Advantages of jettied construction. The overhang helps to stop the upper floor from sagging.

lays on the earth in a shallow trench. Above this are the sillbeams. These have the studs framed into them at the bottom and into the wall plates at the bottom. If the building has two storeys these studs are slotted into the summer or bressummer between the two storeys. In this case the bressumer will carry the floor joists of the upper floor. In the earlier buildings of this kind the studs were close together. In time and as timber became more expensive and more difficult to come by, the distance between the studs became greater.

In many cases jettying was used. This was really the projection of the upper storey beyond the one below it. Usually jettying was used where houses faced one another across a road, but it could also be employed on the flanks of the house or even at the back. Jettying was, in fact, a safety measure for the upper storey's weight hung over the outside wall or walls and helped to prevent that storey sagging in the middle. In early examples of jettying the end of the jetties were sometimes concealed behind fascia boards. This is a point which builders repairing such property will do well to remember. It also meant that rain water would shed off the roof rather further from the house — an important point in the days when there was no damp course.

Timber framed houses needed some kind of weather proofing. The most common form was wattle and daub which was used extensively for infilling

14   A timber framed building which shows how builders built in yester-year.

the panels. The composition of this material varied from one locality to another. Mud and cow dung were considered popular; so was mud and straw. Usually the wattle consisted of either hazel chestnut or cleft oak. In some cases beech was a substitute for the hazel. As time went on brick infilling became popular, especially among those who could afford bricks. The daub was applied to the rough trellis like panels thus created. Today there are many country cottages and even some town houses which have walls of wattle and daub. If such exterior walls are removed they must, of course, be replaced with brick or block walls set in cement.

There are also some mud cottages built of unbaked earth. In such cases turf was often used for the roof. Some of these buildings were lined inside with wattle hurdles. By the late eighteenth century mud was still being used for some thatched houses and cottages. The mixture was, of course, placed between shuttering and rammed well home before being allowed to dry.

Stone buildings
When it comes to buildings few materials look as well as stone. Even the humble cottage achieves a dignity when built in stone. Readers in stone districts are likely to be asked to repair and maintain stone buildings and perhaps they should count themselves fortunate to be able to work in such material. Stone began to be fashionable for ordinary houses and cottages about the middle of the seventeenth century. Before that timer was often used. However stone was replacing timber in the North during the late twelfth and thirteenth century. Previously its use for houses had been confined to such places as Devon and Cornwall and similar stone producing districts. In the early days stone was found on the surface of the ground or on the beds of rivers. Clay mortar was very much in demand, but lime mortar was rare.

In general stone houses relied considerably on the sheer weight of the material. Walls were usually very thick; outside walls being perhaps three to four feet thick. In the mountains the walls of many cottages consisted of dry stone walls. Later many of these were plastered over. Usually such buildings had little or no foundations. They simply stood on the earth.

Stone buildings are built in one of several ways the cheapest being rubble set at random. Usually the corners of buildings were set with stones which have been dressed for the sake of stability. Another way was to use rubble but bring it to course. There was also snecked or squared rubble and squared rubble brought to course. Then there was course squared rubble and polygonal rubble walling. All these demanded dressed stones at the quoins and jambs. Stone walls brought to course are generally speaking, stronger than walls set at random.

Flint
Flint is used for many of the buildings found in chalk districts. Its use as a

building material goes back to the Iron Age. The Romans made extensive use of flint; so did the Normans. It was used extensively throughout the Middle Ages. By the time Elizabeth I was on the throne and wood was getting scarce it had become the usual material for many types of building. Flints have been used for everything from cathedrals to humble cottages. Flint has also been used for farm buildings.

Flints are made of silica; they are shaped irregularly, are very hard and will fracture because of their brittle nature. They occur in layers of chalk and are almost black on the surface. They tend to have a white rind over the surface. They vary in size and shape very considerably but they split easily. Large flints could be snapped and this was sometimes called 'polling'. The polled faces were roughly dressed to about 100mm square; the knapped faces were turned outwards when building walls. Polled and snapped flints were usually reserved for fine buildings such as churches and large houses, while undressed flints were used for cottages and the like. Many flints were uncoursed, but smaller ones were sometimes set in rough courses. A great deal of mortar was needed and flint walls usually had to be thick, their strength being dependent largely on their mass and the mortar which was used. Usually the quoins, jambs, verges and eves were of dressed stone or, more occasionally, brick. In addition to the true flint building cobbles or pebbles were sometimes used.

Brick

The thirteenth century saw the making of the first English bricks. Of course the Romans had used bricks but these were cut to size from a clay slab and, anyway, many of these were probably imported. Roman bricks can be seen in the Abbey at St Albans. When the Abbey was built many years after the Romans left, the monks went down the hill to the site of the old Roman city and carried off the bricks to build what is now the cathedral.

Variations in the colour of bricks is one of their most attractive features. The colour depends mainly on the kind of clay from which they are baked. The position of individual bricks in the kiln when firing takes place also alters the colour. The bricks exposed to the greatest heat tend to be the darkest. There is usually some iron in brick clays and this produces red bricks of different shades. In the old days the Midlands and West produced bricks of deep red although each district had its own colouring. The shales of coal seams in the North produced even redder bricks. The clays of the Weald produce particularly beautiful bricks. Some clays contain a good deal of lime; these produce a yellowish brick and are made from Gault. Suffolk whites are liked by many people while Oxford and Berkshire produce grey bricks.

There is another book in this series concerned with bricks and brickwork and for this reason it is not proposed to deal with bricks in any great detail here. But a word should be said about the bonds which occur in older

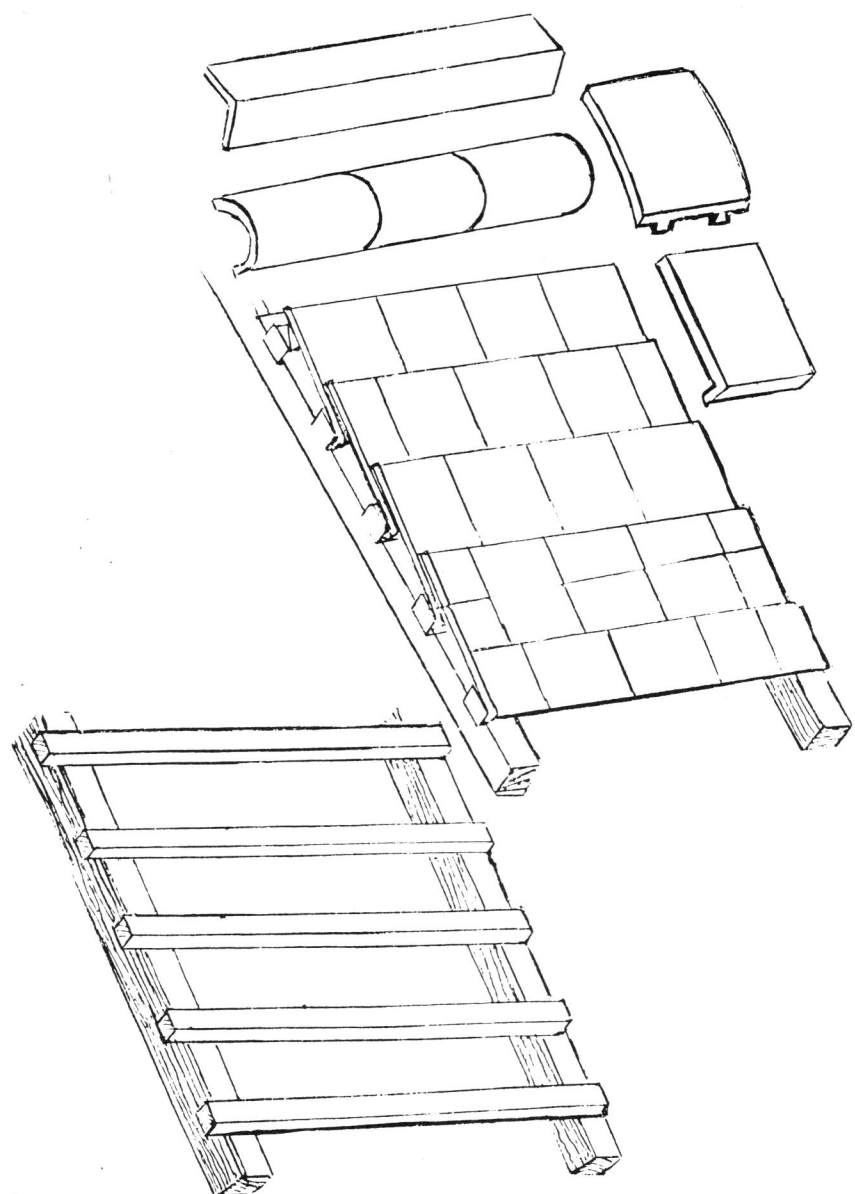

15 Tiles and ridge tiles are often neglected. So are the battens on the roof. The framework is shown here and a section of roof which has been tiled.

properties built before cavity walls came into fashion. Many readers may have occasion to carry out remedial work on brickwork and so need some knowledge of bonds.

In 1784 a tax on bricks was imposed and ten years later this tax was increased. The tax was not abolished until 1850. During the time of the tax the size of bricks was increased because it was levied at two shillings and sixpence a thousand. Naturally enough the builders tried experimenting with different bonds to see if they could economise on brick numbers. In this respect they were less than successful. Nevertheless there are several different bonds which the reader is likely to need to be able to repair. These are bonds such as English, English Garden Wall, Flemish, Flemish Garden Wall, Stretcher, Rattrap, Dearne's and Monk (see chapter 4).

General review
In this the opening chapter, we have discussed several things and it is to be hoped that the reader finds that this whets his or her appetite for what is to come. The truth is that today the repairing builder needs to have a variety of skills to tackle the many different kinds of jobs which will be required.

If the builder is asked for some job which is beyond his/her capacity, the best thing to do is to confess that the job is not quite the right cup of tea but that he/she knows someone who is a specialist in that particular field. For example, the customer is unlikely to expect the builder to do thatching or advanced electrical work. Far better to arrange for an expert to come in. The roof provides a good example. No doubt many builders could undertake roofing and make a good job of it. There there are specialists in roofing and, if the work is extensive it may be far better to call in a roofing contractor to do the work. Never be afraid to say that you prefer to get someone else to undertake some kind of specialist work.

Obviously most of the work a jobbing builder is likely to be asked to undertake will be on houses built during the reign of Queen Victoria and today. It is astonishing how much repair work is needed on houses built since the end of the first world war. The illustrations make this point. Many readers will want to maintain and repair houses, flats and bungalows of this period.

Chapter 2
DEALING WITH DAMP AND DECAY

Damp and decay are two of the worst enemies of well maintained buildings. They cause wood to rot and bricks to crumble. If untreated they can be responsible for structural decay as well as for dampness. It is also important to ensure that heat does not escape from the buildings. The subject of insulation will receive attention elsewhere in this book. There are several important checks to be carried out when looking for signs of dampness in the house and these will be discussed below.

The roof area
Where is dampness likely to occur? There are many places. Let us start by considering the roof. And for all practical purposes we may assume that this is either tiles or slate.

A cracked chimney pot may cause dampness. So may defective flaunching arounds its base. The chimney stack may have defective pointing or, worse, it may be in danger of collapsing. There may be leaking gutters or these may be blocked causing overspill of water. The downpipe may be split and leaking. There may also be some penetration of rain water around the windows or eroded and dislodged pointing on the walls. In the walls there may be choked airbricks or these may have got buried. In either a solid or suspended timber floor there may be damp proof courses which have become bridged.

Inside the house, in the loft, the cistern or pipes may be leaking. Or there may be leaking plumbing in the bathroom. Showers may be giving trouble; so may the w.c. or a basin. Plenty of things can go wrong in the kitchen, the sink, washing machine, dishwasher.

So far we have discussed the outside of the house and the inside. But there is more to be considered. In solid wall houses damp may come through the solid wall. It may also come through cavity wall houses. When such houses are built too much mortar may fall down between the two sets of bricks so that moisture from the outside wall may find its way to the inside one. If the wire struts between the two walls have not been put in correctly moisture may cross there and go into the inner wall. There is also the possibility that if cavity walls are filled with insulating material; moisture may, in some cases, bridge this. So there are many ways in which dampness may enter a house. The only thing to do is to examine the case in question, then decide on the appropriate treatment.

The chimney
A damp house has a distinctive smell; it smells musty and is obviously not right. Let us start at the roof. The chimney pot may be defective. But this is not necessarily obvious from ground level. Examine the chimney with the aid of binoculars before going up on the roof. Also look carefully at the chimney stack. Even if the chimney itself is sound there may be a defect in the flaunching which embeds the pot to the roof. A chimney pot can be very

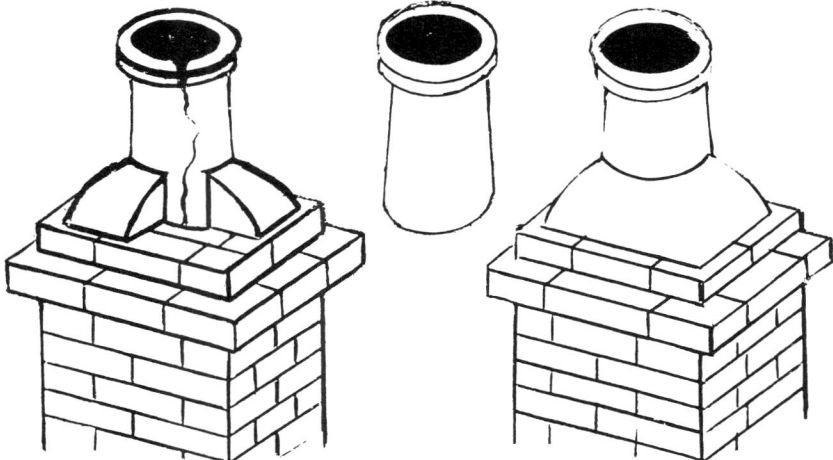

16   Chimney pots are often neglected. But frost and wind can wreck them and eventually they may fracture. Examine them to see if they are all right.

heavy and if it becomes necessary to take it down the best plan is to pass a rope through it before attempting to lower it to the ground. Obviously it is important to use a ladder equipped with a tubular ridge hook as this is the safest form of ladder which can be used for this kind of work. If no such ladder is available secure a shorter ladder to the longer one and let this short ladder trail down the other side of the roof. Or get a mate to stand on the lower rung of the ladder when ever you are on it. There should always be three or four rungs higher than the ridge beam when you are using it. But to return to the chimney.

Examine the pointing in the stack. This pointing may need to be renewed. If the condition of the stack is very bad it will have to be taken down and renewed. On the other hand if the chimney is no longer in use it may be best to remove the stack and fill in the space left in the roof with tiles. Should you decide to cap the chimney make sure you leave some ventilation holes in the fireplace which it served. Do not attempt to seal the chimney so that it gets no air.

Damp patches appearing on the walls can indicate that there is something wrong in the stack area. These patches are usually fairly dark in colour but not so dark that they can be mistaken for the disfigurement which can occur when damp wood is used for the stove. If you burn damp wood you create a build-up of tar like substance inside the chimney which gradually perculates through the wall and discolours the chimney breast inside the house. Such staining is very difficult to remove or, indeed, to cover up.

Tiles and slates
While we are still in the roof area we should consider the state of the tiles or slates. If any of these are damaged they should be replaced. In some cases the slates or tiles will merely have slipped and here they will only need replacing. If the roof is double lap or plain tiles use pieces of flat timber to lift the tiles in the course above the one being lifted. This will enable you to release the nibs of the tiles needing to be replaced. After this use a bricklayers trowel to lift the broken or misplaced tile. Should the tile be held by nails work it loose by moving it about while prising it up with the tip of the trowel. If it is very firmly attached use a slateripper to cut out the nails. Usually the tiles in every fourth row are nailed but in exposed positions every tile may be nailed to prevent the wind lifting it. Handle tiles carefully; they are heavier than they look.

Single lap tiles are replaced quite easily. Fix each such tile with one or two aluminium nails onto the batten in the roof. Clay pantiles are usually just hung on the battens. If they become misplaced in a storm use a masonry drill to drill holes in them at the top and fix with aluminium nails.

Occasionally there may be trouble with ridge tiles. Should these still be bedded firmly but with the joints between them cracked and broken you should be able to repair these joints with non-hardening mastic or thick bitumen pointed into the joint with a trowel. Where however the ridge tile is loose it must be removed and embedded onto a mix of mortar. This mix should consist of Portland cement (one part) and four parts of sharp sand. The tiles should be soaked in water before being replaced and the mix should be placed along the tiles at their edges. Also run the mortar along the joints.

If hip tiles need replacing they should be treated like ridge tiles. Usually a hip tile is prevented from slipping down the roof by a hip iron. If this is missing or in bad condition use a new one. This should be a galvanized hip iron screwed to the foot of the hip rafter with non, rusting screws. The open end may be filled with small pieces of tile in mortar. Bonnet hip tiles may have a top fixing with aluminium nails. The exposed tail is hidden by the mortar.

A slate roof may be more trouble to repair because it may not always be possible to match the slates. They come in various sizes; if the size you require is not available you may have to buy larger slates and cut these down. Use an old slate as a guide to the size required. Score the slate to be cut on both sides with a trowel. With a sharp edged trowel chop half way along. Turn over the slate and chop again, but this time from the other end — until the two chopped lines meet. Do not try to snap a slate.

If you replace a single slate be careful not to damage other neighbouring slates. You will be able to remove a slate if the fixing nails have corroded through but otherwise you will need to use a slate ripper. To do this slide the claw of the ripper around the nails under the slate. When you have the ripper round the nail, pull it to break the nail and then withdraw the slate carefully. The fixing holes of a slate are under the slate above so you cannot nail down a single replacement slate. Instead you need to use a strip of lead about 250mm wide with one end of which you should nail to the batten between the nails of the two exposed slates.

Then — very carefully — lift the edge of the slate above and slide in the replacement slate lining it up with the adjacent slates. Then bend the lead strip's free end so that it holds the replacement slate in place.

To renew ridge slates, which require bedding in mortar, mix a mortar of one part cement to three or four parts of sand. Place this mortar along the ridge and make the surface slightly rough. Then put the ridge slates on the mortar and tap them in with the trowel, making sure that they are level with adjacent slates. Obviously you will have removed any old slates which are damaged and you will have cleaned away old mortar from the top courses of roofing slates. If you are using any of your ridge slates again make sure you chip away any of the old mortar still adhering to them. Should it be necessary to fit the whole of the ridge it may well be more economical to use ridge tiles rather than slates.

If large areas of a roof have to be repaired build a scaffold and use crawling boards so that you can work safely. Whether you work with tiles or slates you should use a masonry drill. Some people hammer a nail through a slate, but it is safer to drill a hole first. Always remember that slate is essentially very fine grained metamorphic rock which cleaves easily and perfectly in one direction but which also flakes and sometimes splits across the grain. Although most slate is grey there are considerable variations in colour depending on where the slate was quarried. If any roof battens need

Victorian house

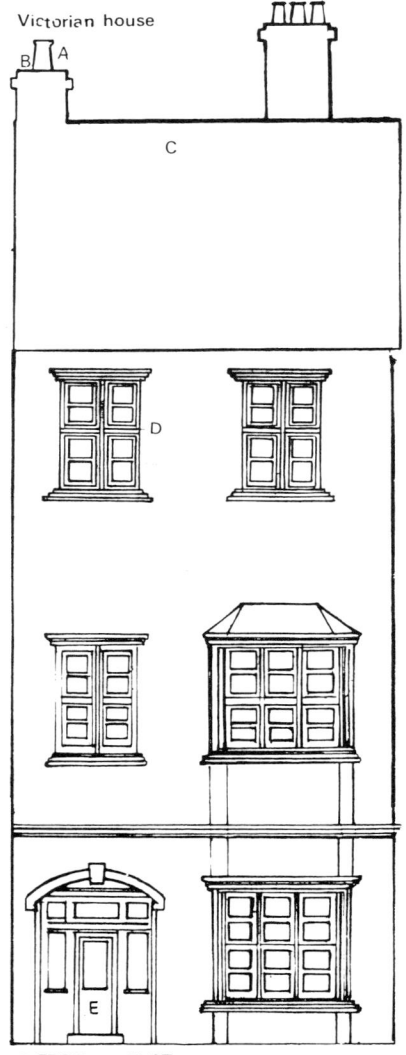

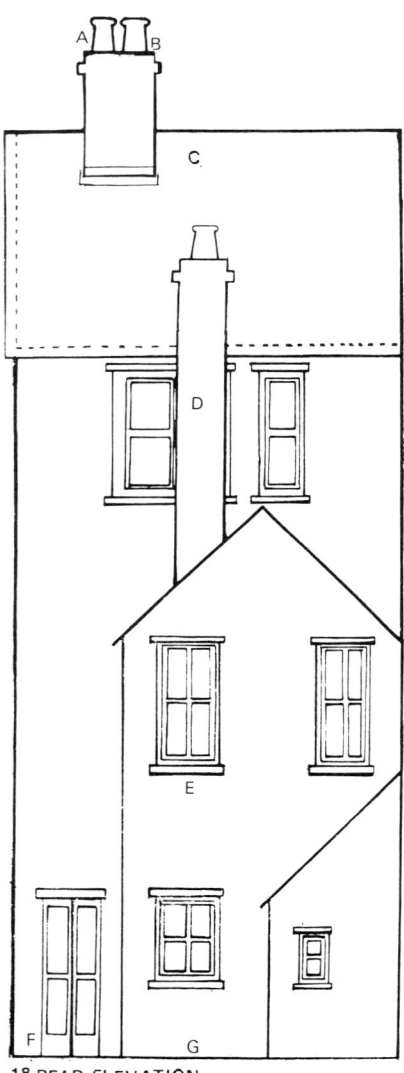

17 FRONT ELEVATION

A Chimney pot — is it broken?
B Flaunching — is it in good order?
C Are any of the roof tiles misplaced or broken?
D Does wet get in through the window frames?
E Does the door fit properly?

18 REAR ELEVATION

A Is the chimney pot all right?
B Is the flaunching sound?
C What about the roof tiles or slates?
D A tall stack — is it in good order?
E Do the windows leak?
F Does the door fit properly?
G Is there a damp proof course and, if so, what is its condition?

renewing saw through these at a diagonal and nail fresh timber to the rafters.

To fix slates begin at the eaves with short slates. Should the job be in the middle of a row slide the first new slate below the last overlapping slate, making sure that the holes are over the centre of the batten. Drive a nail through this hole into the batten. The rest of the slates in the row should be butt-joined. Line up the upper edges and fix each slate with two nails.

Apart from tiles and slates on the roof there can be trouble caused by leaking gutters. These may well be responsible for damp and decay and so, consequently, they merit mention here. Usually the guttering will only be blocked with fallen leaves or other debris. In such a case it must be cleaned out thoroughly and perhaps repainted inside. But guttering can also split; so can down pipes. In such cases walls can become soaked and then the damp patches can appear inside the house. When cleaning gutters also make sure that there are no old birds nests in the down pipes. With tiled roofs gutters can become blocked with sediment and moss. To clen gutters should should have a ladder which extends some three or four rungs above them. For the sake of safety you should lash the ladder to a ring bolt screwed into the fascia board holding the guttering.

Before leaving the roof area there is one kind of maintenance job which should be considered. If there appears to be dampness in the roof look carefully at the flashing around the chimney. This may well be the cause of the trouble. Flashing is used to create a water tight junction between the stack and the roof. If it is defective rain water may come in spoiling the chimney breast and walls below. Should the fault prove to be decayed mortar you should rake out this and then replace the lead flashing. This done insert fresh mortar. The flashing may be lead, zinc, aluminium or a bituminius material. The older the house the more likely it is to be lead. Houses built later may have flashing of an asbestos/bituminius material. In some very old houses you may find a cement mortar fillet where there ought to be flashing.

If the damp has caused patches on the ceilings, walls or chimney breasts inside the house, put right the damage by pushing the flashing back in place and repointing with cement mortar. Also inside the house apply at least two coats of a good sealer and line the walls/ceilings with aluminium foil using a bitumen/rubber adhesive to hold this in place. Then stick a good quality lining paper over the top. Should the flashing be in such bad condition that it cannot be used again, use it as a pattern to cut a fresh one.

Walls

These are the main places where there is likely to be roof trouble. Let us now consider the walls. We have already discussed damp from defective gutters and downpipes.

But there are other possible causes of damage by dampness in walls. It should be remembered that walls can be of two kinds — solid and cavity. Older houses have solid walls but houses built more recently have cavity walls in which there are really two walls. These inner and outer walls are separated by a 50mm cavity across which moisture is not supposed to pass. Sometimes the inner wall is made of blocks rather than bricks. Because the blocks are larger than bricks they save valuable time in the building stages. The two walls are connected either with metal stays or with wire. Today wire is probably the more popular. In the middle of the stay the wire is looped down so that, if any damp should to along the wire it will drip downwards instead of reaching the inner wall. Thus it will land between the two courses of brick/block and below the damp proof course.

In some cases brickwork becomes soaked with rain and becomes porous. Some of this dampness may get transmitted to the inner wall and so will cause damp patches to appear. Damp walls are difficult to cure. However

19 Victorian house side elevaton.
Are the walls sound?
Is there a damp proof course?

when the walls dry out there are several things which can be done. Although they are not waterproof both rough cast and pebble dash are treatments for the outside of walls which are likely to prove beneficial. So is ordinary cement rendering. The surface thus created may usefully be treated with either a cement or stone based paint or, alternatively, with a good quality outdoor exterior grade emulsion.

Of course gloss paint or a bitumen paint would be fine as far as waterproofing is concerned, but these paints are not necessarily attractive for walls (especially the latter) and they would keep any dampness present in the wall inside it if they were to be used. Some liquid sealers can be painted on walls which will help and which can be painted over or even papered afterwards. Where a wall has become damp because the decorative finish of it has cracked, cut out the damage cracks and fill these with mortar and then use fresh rendering. Should the damp persist try more painting with the exterior grade emulsion already mentioned.

For damp interior walls you may be able to line them with aluminium foil or waterproof laminated paper. This will not get rid of the damp, but it should seal it in so that it is not a disfigurement.

Another possible source of damp in walls is the moisture which can gain access from window and door frames. The first thing to be done is to make sure that windows and doors fit properly. If they do not they must be repaired as quickly as possible.

It is quite possible that a house is suffering from rising damp. Rising damp means that either there is no damp proof course or that, if there has been such a course, it has become ineffective. Years ago houses did not have damp courses and this may well be the trouble, especially if there are solid brick walls. Rising damp comes from the ground and takes the form of damp patches at or near the skirting on the ground floor. If the trouble is not serious it may be treated with a damp repellant in liquid form on the outside and also on the inside. It is also possible to have holes drilled in the wall around the house to take a silicone injection in the brickwork. This should be done just where the damp proof course would be if it were there. The silicone should seep through the brickwork to a depth of some 225 mm and should form a barrier which should prevent dampness getting higher. See the appropriate chapter for details of laying a damp proof course. In general there are several ways of doing this.

A liquid can be injected into the wall which should diffuse throughout the brickwork to form a damp proof barrier. The liquid can be injected under pressure into the wall through a series of holes drilled outside. Alternatively it can be placed in bottles connected to the holes by pipes. Within a few days the liquid will have penetrated the wall. An alternative is to use the electro osmosis process which relies on the difference between the electrical charge between the wall and the earth which causes damp to rise. Here electrodes are fitted into the wall and linked with a copper strip

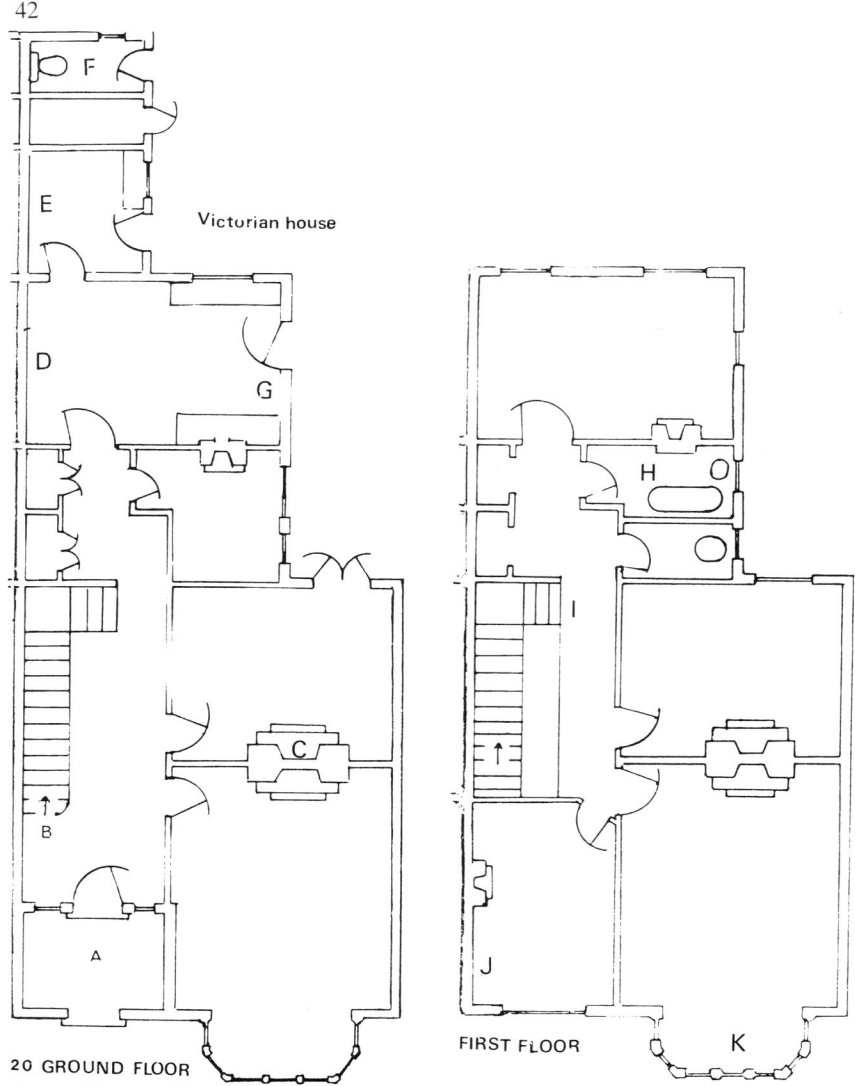

Victorian house

20 GROUND FLOOR

FIRST FLOOR

Ground floor and first floor.
A Is the porch damp?
B Are the stairs sound?
C What about the fireplaces and chimneys?
D Is the kitchen stove satisfactory?
E Is the coal cellar damp?
F Is the WC in order?
H Is everything right in the bathroom?
I Is the landing floor and the top of the stairs sound?
K Does the bay window leak?

which is linked to an electrode in the ground. The very small electric charges in the wet wall can then be discharged down into the earth.

There is an alternative method whereby holes are drilled into the wall from either the inside or outside of the house. Ceramic tubes which are porous are then fitted into the holes and bonded with porous mortar before being fitted with a protective cap. Moisture is drawn through the porous tubes which then evaporates.

But perhaps the best way for the reader to cure rising damp is to cut through the existing wall — a little at a time — with a power saw and insert a damp proof course as the work progresses. The usual dpc strip is suitable but do not attempt to build your dpc of slates as these will be too thick to go into the cut you make. Finish off with mortar.

To deal with damp in the house is obviously important because if it is not attended to promptly, it will encourage wither dry or wet rot or both. Where rot takes hold the affected timber must be cut out and destroyed. This can prove a complicated and costly job. But before the tumber can be treated you will have to decide on what kind of rot has set in. It should be possible for the builder to deal with either wet or dry rot, but remember that there are specialist firms which undertake such work and it may well be best to get in touch with one of these.

Dry rot
For timber to rot it must be fairly wet and starved of air. Dry rot spreads very rapidly and it must be dealt with as soon as it is discovered. Wet rot attracts wet or damp timber. Wet rot is far more likely to occur than dry rot, but it is usually not quite as serious. Dry rot, on the other hand, can easily transfer itself to dry timber from damp timber. In this respect it is worse than wet rot. Dry rot is caused by a fungus which starts on damp wood and then attacks dry timber.

It will spread throughout the building if it is not treated. At first matted strands of fungus appear on the surface of the timber. In fact the early stages of dry rot usually produce a silver grey web which may be tinged with yellow or lilac. If humidity is high the fungus may grow rapidly so that it soon looks like a soft cushion. This is usually white and has a texture not unlike cottonwool. In some cases the edges turn bright yellow, especially if they come into contact with air. They may also do this when exposed to light. If the fungus is still growing and conditions are very damp water may form in globules. In due course the wood which has been attacked becomes decayed; it gets darker in colour and much lighter in weight. Finally it reached the stage where it crumbles in the hand. In very bad cases a fruiting body may appear. At first this is likely to be a pale grey colour with white edges. The middle of this fruiting body may be corrugated. Later there may well be a sprinkling of rusted spores. When this happens there may also be a strong smell of mushrooms.

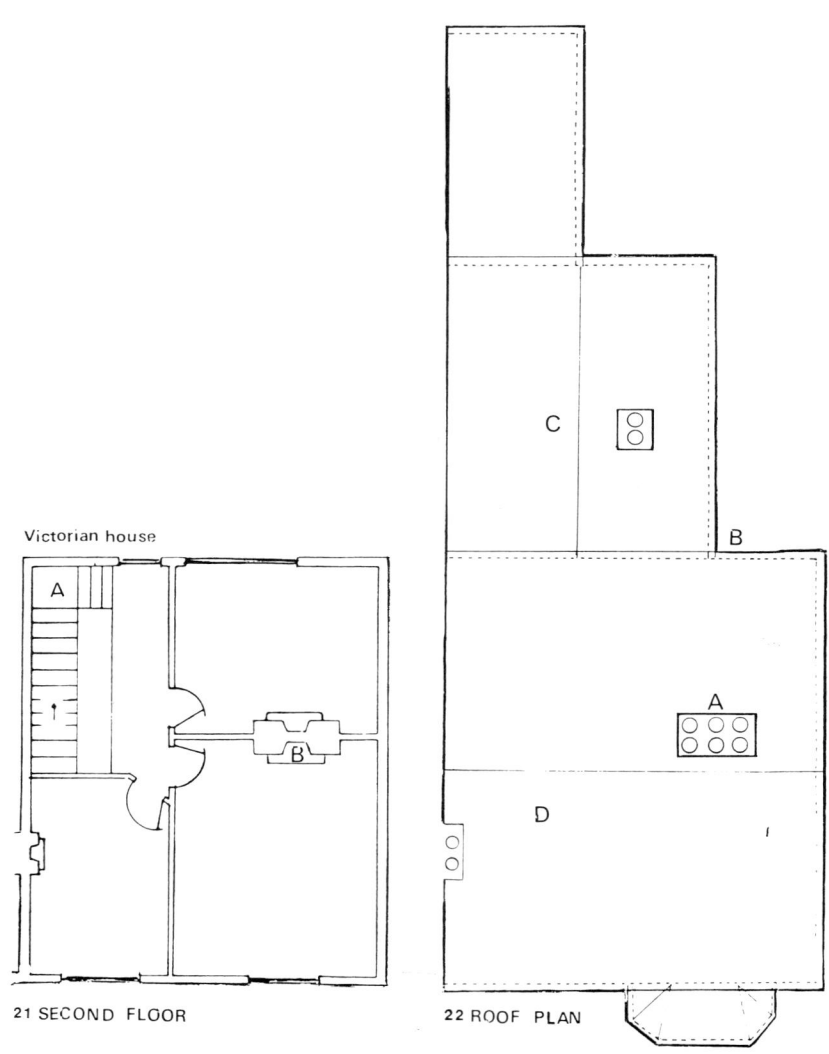

Victorian house

21 SECOND FLOOR

22 ROOF PLAN

21 A Is this part of the staircase sound?
    B Is this fireplace ever used and should it be removed?
22 A Are the chimneys in good order?
    B Is the guttering all right?
    C What are the ridge tiles like?
    D What is the condition of the rest of the roof?

One kind of dry rot called Merulius lacrymans which requires moist, warm and windless conditions and untreated timber with a moisture content of over 22 per cent, attacks the cellulose in such timber breaking it down to carbon dioxide and water. Thus the timber loses its strength and develops cuboidal splitting so that it becomes dry and powdery. The penetration of the material being attacked then begins. The hyphae of the fungus produce enzymes which digest adjacent damp timber. The strands may penetrate through brickwork or stonework following the damp and searching for fresh timber to attack. The fungus can produce a fleshy fruiting body within a year when conditions are ideal for it but such quick growth may be considered somewhat unusual.

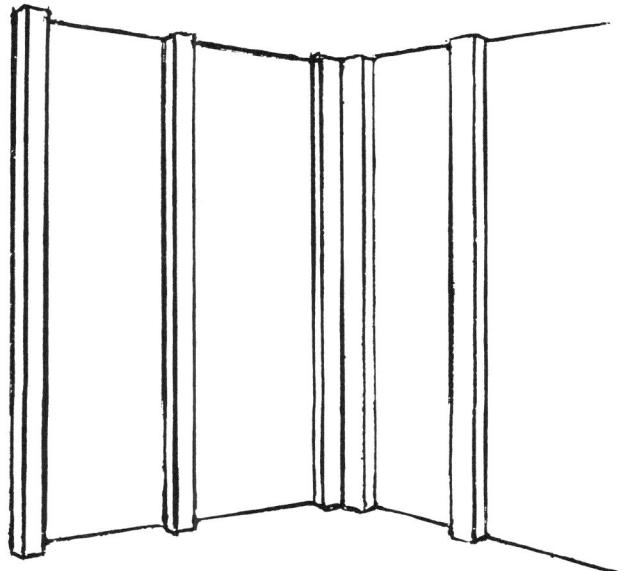

23   Damp walls can be treated in several ways, one of which is to apply battens and then hardboard. Here a corner of a room awaits the board, but before this is applied it may be desirable to put in cross pieces horizontally.

Cellar fungus, such as coniphora cerebella, is one of the wet rot fungi which feeds on damp softwood. When attacked the wood loses weight and strength and finally collapses. This fungus usually needs more moisture than a dry rot fungus. Here the fruiting body is an oval greenish and rather flat sporophore. Dark brown strands soon develop on the surface. This fungus loves cellars and other damp, dark places which do not get much fresh air. Another wet rot fungus is Poria vaporial or pore fungus; this feeds on damp softwood. It is less fussy about temperature conditions than some fungi. The hyphae or root system has a fan shaped pattern over the timber and is white. This fungus thrives in mines as well as damp buildings.

Dry rot fungus may have roots which convey water and the fungus itself to other timbers nearby even when these are dry. So it will not be sufficient to cut out the affected timber. If other timber nearby is likely to have been affected it must be cut out and disposed of at once. The strands of fungus will very likely have reached nearby woodwork. Such strands sometimes pass through brickwork or stone and other materials.

Once you have decided that there is dry rot in a building check all the timbers thoroughly. Look for damp which may have entered through the roof, walls or floor. Examine the damp proof course and look for rising damp in the floors and lower sections of the walls. Check for damp places at the windows and doors. Cut back all affected timber by rather more than a metre from the trouble.

Remember that the first signs of dry rot may be a spread of mycelium. This may be grey, brown or white sheets of threads. These will probably be of a cotton wool texture. This means that the mycelium spores of the dry rot have grown on timber which has probably had more than 20% moisture content. In extreme cases there are fruiting bodies which look something like toadstool caps. If these are not removed they will produce more spores and so the dry rot will progress to other timber. Dry rot is fairly easy to detect. Rooms begin to smell musty and they remind you of mushrooms growing. Paintwork begins to flake off and timber may become warped. Longitudinal splits appear in timber which may also crack across the grain. On plaster damp patches may appear where fungi is attacking the walls. Skirting boards may become warped and distorted. If you are uncertain, lift a few floor boards and see if you can find any traces of rot beneath them. Timber which is decayed is usually brown and will crumble easily in the hand.

Where there is dry rot the following procedures should be followed. Timber showing signs of dry rot must be cut away at least a metre beyond the affected part. Also remove plaster work such as the ceiling and wall which may have been penetrated by the dry rot. The strands may have penetrated adjacent brickwork or plaster or even concrete; rake out all mortar joints. You may find spores on ground beneath suspended floors and if you do, then remove the top six inches of this soil and burn it. Then sterilize the affected areas with a fungicide by spraying the walls, ceiling and floor. Also spray any timber which remains within two metres of the attack. Do not neglect nooks and crannies and such things as pipework within about two metres. Saturate the whole area with fungicidal fluid applying this to all timber, brickwork, blocks, concrete and earth. Apply at the rate recommended by the manufacturer of the product and use it very carefully. If possible use a fairly coarse spray — perhaps a hydraulic pump. Alternatively a knapsack garden spray may prove useful.

Timber for replacing affected woodwork must be thoroughly well seasoned and dry. Give it a couple of coats of wood preservative which complies with British Standards specification. Soak the sawn ends of timber in the fungicide for several minutes before attempting to replace the timber. If there is any rubber coated cable near the affected timber first paint this with polyurethane paint to ensure that the fungicide does not damage the rubber. Today, of course, electric cable is usually plastic coated. A rendering of zinc oxychloride plaster should guard against further attack. Of the several different kinds of fungi which represent dry rot Merulis lacrymans is probably the most common.

Wet rot

It is usually much easier to deal with wet rot than with dry rot. Obviously the site of the trouble has to be examined carefully to pin point the cause of it. The most common cause of wet rot is cellar fungus. Wet rot does not attack dry timber. When it has been eradicated treat the wood with a preservative in case any of the wood is still sufficiently damp for any stray spores to grow again. Wet rot usually takes the form of staining the timber black or at least a very dark colour. There may also be dark brown threads. Wet rot fungus will not thrive on timber which is dry. But there may be cracks with the grain; there may also be some cross grain cracking but the cubes are usually smaller than those formed by dry rot. There may be patches of yellow or brown in affected timber.

When the timber has dried out wet rot fungus stops growing. Nor does it transfer itself to dry timber. So, in addition to removing all affected timber you must be sure that the rest of the timber has dried out thoroughly. Cut the timber back until you reach wood which is still in good condition, make sure you have eliminated the dampness and dried out the wood and then treat the timber with a good preservative taking care to apply this in accordance with the maker's instructions. If the surface of the affected timber is badly decayed scrape this away and, having removed the decayed wood, then apply more preservative giving at least two coats. When examining new timber look for grey blue patterns on soft wood. In itself such patterns are not serious but they may indicate dampness which might become more serious.

So, if possible, refrain from buying such timber. This of course applies to softwoods. If you have to buy timber of this kind coat it with preservative once you have brushed off the fungus. You may also care to give such timber a primer if you do not expect to use it for some time.

Sources of extraneous damp

Before leaving the general subject of dampness in buildings there are two or three points which should be tidied up. So far we have discussed damp in the roof area, the walls and dry and wet rot. But there are also other forms of moisture which deserve some mention. One of these is water which may come from sources indoors. These include dripping taps, sinks which are blocked up, malfunctioning showers, the w.c. and like matters. Obviously there are two jobs to be done here. One is to remedy the defect and the other is to treat whatever has been damaged by the wet getting in. Even a central heating system may give trouble and leak.

The other source of annoyance is rising damp from floors which have not got proper damp proof courses. Here again the job has to be divided into two stages. One is curing the trouble by removing any timber which has got damp and started to rot and the other is to remedy the defect so that it does not occur again. Some reference has already been made to installing a damp proof course and no further comment is called for at this stage, except to say that providing a damp proof course for a house which has not got one is likely to be a big job. Remember that there can be vertical damp proof courses as well as horizontal ones.

The other point is concerned with the leakage of water pipes etc within the house. Of course, water can also enter a house from a leaking roof, burst pipes or even water mains. Usually this kind of trouble is spotted early and timber is unlikely to become soaked over a period of time. Nevertheless, considerable damage can be done to interior decorations to say nothing of the inconvenience of having such things happen.

Chapter 3
CONDENSATION, WOOD PESTS AND THE NATURE OF TIMBER

Condensation

In the last chapter we discussed dry and wet rot and we saw that rising damp is what happens when damp rises by the capillary action of ground moisture. The extent to which it can be troublesome depends on how much damp there is and of the nature of the material making the wall. Rising damp often leaves a band at the top of efflorescence which consists of powdery salts which are usually white in colour. Below this band the wall becomes discoloured; it may look dark and there may be blackish mould growths. Wall paper may peel and plaster may flake off. Wet rot does not attack dry timber and consequently it is easier to get rid of it. There is also penetrating rain and moisture which may enter through defective roofs or leaking guttering and down pipes etc. In addition to these things there is condensation.

When damp air hits a cold surface the moisture in it produces condensation. Perhaps the best example of this is when dampness hits the window and "rivers" of moisture run down the glass to the bottom. On damp, foggy days, it is difficult to prevent condensation except with double glazing and in very cold weather the trouble is likely to be at its worst. Condensation not only causes misting on windows; it may also be recognised by beads of moisture dripping from pipes or the w.c. pipe leading to the cistern. It attacks chimneys, especially where damp fuel is used such as, for example, unseasoned wood. In such cases there may be condensation inside the chimney leading to a build up of black tar-like products. These deposits are dangerous because they may produce black marks on the outside of the chimney breast and, in extreme cases, may also block up the chimney causing it to smoke. If black marks appear they are very difficult indeed to eradicate and so are apt to spoil the decoration of a room.

So damp, muggy weather is likely to produce just the kind of conditions such pests need and in some climates the damp is more likely to be caused by either the ingress of rain water or rising damp. On the other hand a cold, crisp day will often promote condensation not only on the glass in windows but also on other materials such as plastered walls. There will probably be condensation on almost any hard, smooth surface. Condensation may be said to occur wherever warm air containing a lot of moisture vapour strikes a cold surface. The air is cooled and is no longer able to hold so much moisture so it deposits some of it on the cold surface. When streams of moisture form and run down the window there is some danger of the window frames rotting. Mildew may appear on clothes and curtains as well as walls.

Good ventilation is a must for such a situation. Here the aim should be to carry the warm, damp air away and replace it with fresh, drier air from outside. On cold winter days the air drawn into a house may only contain half the moisture of the warm air inside. Ventilation through cracks at windows and doors may replace some of the warm air but such cracks will lose a great deal of heat. They should be sealed and when they have been draughtproofed, provide proper ventilation. This may require an advanced sophisticated ventilation system or it may mean simply opening a window. Do not keep the window open for more than a few minutes each time you ventilate or you will lose valuable heat.

Tips on living with condensation
The builder with a client who is troubled by condensation may well be able to help by talking to him or her. After all condensation is something we have to live with and any tips which can be passed on to the householder should be welcome. So here are a few practical points. Dry cloths outside or in a tumble dryer vented to the outside. With saucepan lids on simmer vegetables gently. Use an electric kettle which switches off automatically and does not make unnecessary steam. If the heating system has a separate control for hot water so much the better.

Keep the kitchen door closed when cooking and the bathroom door closed when using the bath. If possible use domestic hot water at a temperature of about 60C or less; if the water is stored at this temperature it will save heating bills as well as reduce condensation. During the night a person breathes out some 0.3 litres of water vapour. The average family may well produce some 5 to 15 litres of water each day. Keep the house well ventilated with windows open for part of the day. Even in the winter the fresh air entering the house is likely to contain less damp than warm damp air already in the house.

An extraction fan in the kitchen to remove the moisture laden warm air may help. Such a fan should be placed as high up as possible in the wall. A cooker in a kitchen is helpful because it sucks some of the warm air up and sends it outside. Wall insulation is also some use, especially if it takes the form of a thin layer of expanded polystyrene which comes in rolls. Should there be any condensation in the walls it may be possible to put in an air brick in the wall to improve the ventilation.

Wood pests

Although damp, wet and dry rot has been discussed already in this book together with condensation, the subject of wood pests has not yet received attention. So let us consider woodworm. Woodworm is the larva of Anobium punctatum and is of the family of Anobiidae. This is the common furniture beetle which sometimes attacks timber in building and seems to be particularly fond of plywood. The tiny white eggs which are oval in shape are laid in small cracks in wood. The larvae burrow into and through the wood, moulting occasionally and pupating from time to time. Then the adult beetle emerges in Spring leaving tiny holes which are visible. The life cycle may take several years to complete. Preparations are sold which are supposed to kill the pest and, indeed, they probably do. Unfortunately however the task of squirting each hole is very tedious.

Termites which are sometimes called white ants are fortunately not troublesome in this country. But since some copies of this book may go elsewhere, they are mentioned here. Termites are extremely destructive throughout the tropics, North America, Australia and parts of Continental Europe. They attack trees, timber, and food crops as well as rubber and some plastics. There are two principal groups: Subterranean termites and Drywood termites.

The Subterranean termites called Termopsidae are the damp wood pests; the Termitidae termites dwell in damp wood; the moist wood termites are the Rhinotermitidae termites. All these live in colonies in large mounds and they make mud tunnels. In this country termites are not a problem but it is a very different story in many other countries.

The other group is the dry wood termites and they are called kalotermitidae. They spend most of their lives in the wood, but the flying adults go off to lay their eggs in cracks in other wood. These termites are particularly troublesome near the coast. Although we are not troubled with termites there are still plenty of other pests to worry about.

The common furniture beetle has already been mentioned briefly. The name is Anobium punctatum. It can destroy either soft wood or hard wood. The larvae of the beetle bores through the wood digesting the cellulose and after two or three years forms a pupal chamber close to the surface. There the larvae change into adult beetles. During the summer they bite their way out of the wood leaving a small, round hole on the surface. When they have mated the females lay their eggs (up to about eighty) in cracks, old flight holes and crevices. The life cycle begins all over again. The eggs hatch and the life cycle can be as short as three years.

The death watch beetle, called Xestobium rufovillosum, is related to the common furniture beetle, but is somewhat larger. Indeed its flight hole is some 3mm in diameter and it produces coarse bore dust. The larvae like decaying oak and, from egg to adult, the life cycle may be as short as four years. However if the wood is dry and sound the larvae may tunnel up to as long as twelve years before pupating. During this time they can do a great deal of damage. In due course the larvae pupate and so turn into beetles. When these emerge from the wood they mate and the life cycle begins all over again. Females lay as many as a couple of hundred eggs. Usually this pest attacks hardwood, but it has been known to destroy decaying softwood. During the flight season there may be a tapping sound which is caused by the head of the beetle. This beetle is often to be found in churches and similar woodwork and the tapping is likely to be a mating call.

The house longhorn beetle or hylotrupes bajulus, is a destructive insect which particularly attacks well seasoned softwood. The eggs are laid in cracks and crevices. In about three weeks the eggs hatch out into larvae or grubs. These tunnel through the wood and they are believed to be capable of eating their own length in a day. When close to maturity they can be as much as 25mm long, so the damage can be very considerable. After some seven years of tunnelling the adult beetle emerges from the wood during the mating season. The flight hole can be up to 10mm long and about 6mm wide. Mated feamles may lay anything up to a couple of hundred eggs. The house longhorn beetle is often found in Surrey and Hampshire. But other counties may also be troubled by it.

There are also wood boring weevils called Euophryum confinel which look rather similar to the common furniture beetle except that it has a long snout. It attacks timber which is already decayed by fungi. Being very prolific this insect may have a couple of two complete life cycles a year. Consequently it does a great deal of structural damage to timber. Weevils prefer sappy timber; their tunnelling makes slot-like galleries in timber.

Fortunately there are well recognised proprietary products which are available for dealing with these pests and the reader should obtain the appropriate one and use it following the instruction carefully. No mention has been made of silverfish which a builder may encounter when working on old property. The presence of silverfish may well indicate a fault in the plumbing producing unwanted dampness. If you find silverfish you should suspect rising damp or perhaps a cracked, leaking pipe. Usually they are found in kitchens, bathrooms and utility rooms containing appliances which use water.

They are attracted by carbohydrate material and warmth. The damage they do to a building is minor but some wallpaper may become discoloured. The best plan is to spray cracks and crevices near plumbing fittings with carbaryl insect powder or an aerosol or use an insecticide for crawling insects. Silverfish belong to the order of Tysanura which includes small silvery primitive wingless Lepisma saccharina and the family Lepismatidae.

In some foreign countries builders have to be careful of such pests as mosquitoes for malaria and yellow fever; fleas for plague; the human louse for typhus; the tsetse fly for sleeping sickness; blood sucking bugs for chayas disease; sansflies for leishmaniasis. In the past various remedies have been tried for such pests. As long ago as 1763 poisonous plant compounds such as ground tobacco was used to kill aphids in France. Other "remedies" such as nicotine, rotenone, petroleum, kerosene, creosote and turpentine have been used during the nineteenth century. In about 1800 several inorganic compounds became popular. These include Paris green, sulfur, Bordeaux mixture, hydrogen agahide, lead and arsenate.

We began this chapter by considering condensation and the various pests which attack wood. Now let us consider the nature of wood itself and not a few ways in which may be cut for building purposes.

The nature of timber

Trees grow by adding a new layer each year. These layers are known as annual growth rings. Each spring the sap ascends from the roots to produce spring wood. During summer carbon dioxide is taken into the plant through its leaves. This thickens the sap which descends in the autumn to thicken the ring. The annual ring occurs in the cambium layer next to the bark. The rings are made up of spring wood and summer wood. Heart wood or Duramen is the inner part of the tree; it is more dense and harder than the rest of the tree and, quite often, it is somewhat darker in colour. The central core of the tree is pith. Around the sap wood layers the timber is not quite so strong as the heart wood. This part of the tree is called the alburnum and is of more recent growth than the heart wood. Medullary rays consist of ribbons of cellular tissue running radially. They go from the pith to the bark. In hardwoods they are usually quite visible.

To prevent shrinkage in finished work timber should be seasoned. In this way as much sap as possible will dry out. The conventional way to season planks and beams is to build them into stacks. Air is allowed to circulate around them by means of wedges placed between the various layers.

The stacks should be protected by a roof over them, but the air must be allowed to blow through them. Boards of about two inches thick require about two years to season properly — more if possible. This applies to hardwoods. The softwoods season rather more quickly. The modern process of seasoning can be speeded up by kiln drying. Preheated warm air is circulated around the timber which is placed in a steam heated chamber; it is stacked in such a way that it does not warp or cockle. The seasoning of timber in this way is a skilled business.

There are two classes of trees — hard and soft woods. Hardwoods are deciduous and shed their leaves every year. Softwoods are coniferous or cone bearing. They shed their needles but otherwise they are evergreens the year round. Most softwoods contain resinous matter while many hardwoods do not. But softwoods have wider annual rings than hardwoods. Softwoods do not have visable medullary rays and their sap wood usually shows less difference between that and the heartwood than is the case with hardwood. Although yellow deal is used extensively in Britain there are, in fact, fewer softwoods in the world than hardwoods. The following are a few notes about woods.

Softwoods
Of the softwoods northern pine is perhaps the most popular. This is also known as Baltic pine, Scotch Fir, yellow fir, red or yellow deal, and various other names. The wood is yellowish to reddish brown in colour. Quality varies considerably. The timber from Archangel had a good reputation for many years and still deserves it. It makes excellent roof timbers, windows, flooring, doors and is useful for all general carpentry.

Douglas fir also known as Oregon pine, British Columbian pine and a few other names, is hard and strong and highly resinous. It is usually reddish brown in colour. This timber has long been used for doors, flooring and panelling. Stains and varnish may be used but there is really too much resin for good paintwork. Douglas fir has been shipped from North America in great quantities.

Pitch pine is also very resinous but it is har, strong and durable. Again it does not paint very well but is fine for varnish. This timber has a good figure for the annual rings are strongly marked. Sometimes used for roof trusses, masts and flooring. It comes from the United States and Canada.

White deal of fir is yellowish or blueish white. It is soft and easily worked and the better qualities have been used for shelves and domestic joinery about the house. Other softwoods of some interest include larch for fencing and telegraph poles. Yew is used mostly by the furniture making trade rather than by builders.

Hardwoods
There are many varieties of oak which are used in building. These include English oak, American, Australian and Japanese. Strength, toughness and durability are the essential characteristics of oak. Its pronounced medullary rays provide the wood with attractive silver grey markings when it is rift sawn. However it contains an acid which attacks iron and lead which it corrodes. It is used extensively for flooring, roof trusses, and beams. Also very popular for window sills.

Mahogany and its near relatives is used for many building purposes. Traditionally it comes from Honduras, Africa, Cuba etc. It is a very decorative hardwood which is extremely popular for doors and general joinery.

Walnut is rather rare today but it is hard and suitable for high class joinery. It is a decorative wood with a good figure.

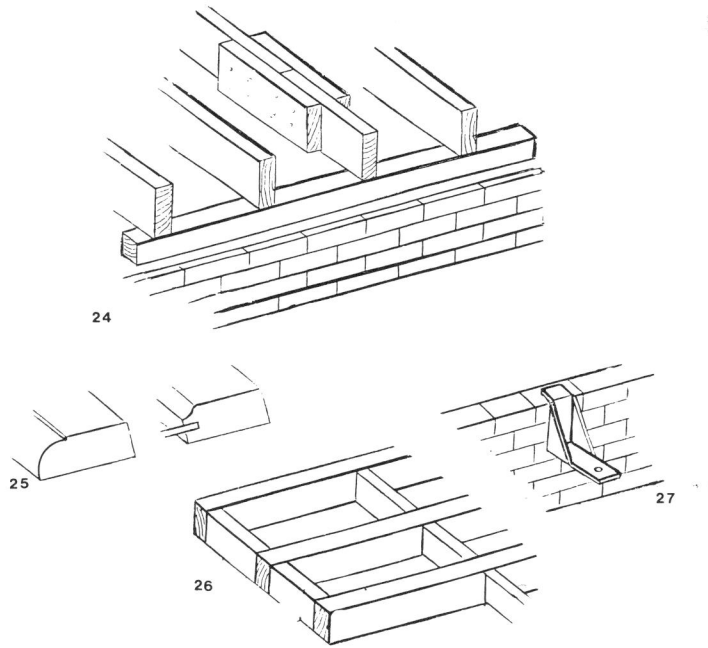

24 Repairing a joist with wood either side. In many cases the ends of joists get attacked by damp or by pests and need to be renewed.
25 When contemplating the joinery of an old house it is as well to remember that mouldings may well be made up of various components.
26 Strengthening a floor can often be done by adding cross pieces in the joists.
27 Steel bracket for the ends of joists to take floor structure. This is sometimes the best way to mend a damaged joist.

Teak has traditionally been used for boat building. It repels water excellently and is often used for garden seats and summer houses. Teak comes from Burma and India. Teak is not particularly easy to work but, because of an oil it contains, resists insects and damp. Teak is used for floors, doors and stair cases and for a great deal of high class joinery.

Converting timber
There are several ways in which a log may be cut up into boards and planks. One of these is just ordinary sawing. It is less wasteful than any other method but it encourages the warping of timber. This tendency to warp is

particularly strong in the pieces cut from close to the outside of the log. Then there is rift or radial sawn timber. This is sawn at right angles to the annual rings. First the log is quarter sawn after which the quarters are sawn up producing rift sawn planks. By producing planks which are cut obliquely across the medullary rays a very decorative figure results. Tangential sawn means cutting planks tangentially to the annual rings. In some woods this produces excellent figuring. Waney edges means cutting planks too large for the log so that some of the rounded tree remains.

Timber defects
It may be useful to list some of the defects which can occur in timber. Heart shakes start from the centre of the log; they are really shrinkage cracks and when there are a number of these they are called star shakes. Knots are hard portions of wood which have produced branches and which have become embedded in the wood during natural growth. Ring shakes follow the path of the annual rings. These shakes are sometimes called cup shakes. Burrs are swellings which are caused by the wood swelling over a wound which might have occurred, for instance, by the breaking of a branch or a sharp blow. Burrs are often regarded as highly decorative in certain woods such as oak or walnut. Twisted grain usually comes from the action of wind on growing trees. Dry and wet rot have already been discussed at some length. So has decay caused by worms and insects. While upset usually means the mal-arranging of fibres which have been injured by crushing or some kind of mechanical shock during the growing stages.

Plywood, blockboard and chipboard
Plywood is a laminated timber consisting of a number of plys stuck together under pressure and heat. The grain of each laminate runs at right angles to the grain of the previous laminate. In this way a very stable product is created as there is very little expansion or contraction due to changes in temperature. For decorative work the outer laminates may be of figured grain. Today a great deal of plywood is resin bonded rather than glued.

Laminated block board has a core of strips of board, the grain of which runs first one way and then the other as shown in the illustration. Sometimes this is called strip board. A laminate is applied either side of the pieces of wood. Usually the better quality block boards have cores of hardwood such as, for example, gaboon. Today more and more chip board is used. This may have plywood or plastic sheet either side on the outside. It is obtainable in various thicknesses and sizes and is very popular with both builders and diy enthusiasts.

Chapter 4
BUILDING MATERIALS

So far we have discussed timber and mentioned some other materials. Now let us consider some other building materials. Since this book is concerned with the repair and maintenance of houses let us pay special attention to those materials most likely to be found in that kind of property.

Aggregate

Aggregates must be clean and there should be no coating of clay or dirt or mould around each piece as this would prevent proper adhesion of the cement. Aggregate varies in size and, for many purposes a medium grade will be required. When aggregate and sand are combined for sale they sometimes called "all in ballast". Most aggregates consist of small stones, but some are made from crushed rock. The exact grade to be chosen will depend on the kind of concrete required.

Cement

Portland cement was invented by Joseph Aspdin, a bricklayer in Leeds in 1824. Since then it has been greatly improved. Chalk or limestone is mixed with clay in proportions of about three to one and with water so that it becomes a creamy liquid or slurry. This is heated to a high temperature in a special type of kiln. This fuses into clinker somewhat similar to coke. When the clinker is cool it is ground into a fine powder and some gypsum may be added to control the time taken for setting. The heat of the kiln makes the chalk combine with the clay to form various chemical compounds which control the setting time. The water also pays an important part in this. Being a hydraulic type of material Portland cement will also harden under water.

Rapid hardening Portland cement is ground far more finely than normal cement. The finer it is ground the more rapidly it will set. As mentioned above there have been great advances in the making of modern Portland cement but this gives an idea of how it started. There are also coloured cements in that there are colouring agents which can be introduced. In addition there is white cement. It should be understood that setting time refers to the time needed for certain chemical reactions to take place between the powder and the water used. Setting time should not be confused with hardening time. The latter refers to the time needed to develop strength in the mortar or concrete being made. It is a mistake to knock up old cement with more water then use it if it has already had several hours in which to mature. This, of course, does not apply to ready mixed stuff which is kept moving while it is being delivered to the site. Ready mix is very useful, but it has to be dealt with as soon as it arrives on the site. In very general terms rapid hardening cement is approximately as strong after four days as ordinary cement would be after something like twenty eight days. Interestingly enough it is true that concrete goes on getting harder and harder; in fact it may go on hardening for some twenty years.

Quick setting Portland cement when used for concrete is useful for work in water which is flowing. Normal setting material would probably be washed away if it were used. To resist corrosion in sea defences Portland blast furnace cement should be used. This is usually a mixture of Portland cement and finely ground slag from iron blast furnaces. This makes it suitable for resisting salt water; it also makes it more fire resistant. Normal Portland cement, quick setting Portland cement and blast furnace cement all take about twenty eight days to reach a good hard state while rapid hardening cement does it is some three to four days.

Cement must be kept very dry. If it becomes damp before use it is likely to go lumpy this means that some of the chemicals have started to set. The resulting material will be slower to set when it is used and it will not be so strong.

Concrete
Having discussed aggregate let us now consider concrete of which there are many kinds. Basically the ingredients consist of cement, sand, aggregate and water. In graded concrete the ballast consists of particles of different sizes. Thus the smaller particles (sand) fill in the crevices between the larger ones and, consequently, less cement is used. Thorough grading produces concrete which is more dense. So its strength and ability to be water tight will be greater. The more the small particles fill up the spaces between the larger ones the better. The size of coarse aggregate varies according to the purpose for which it is to be used. In foundations, for instance, mass concrete as it is called, may have aggregate of stones passing through a two and a half inch mesh, while for reinforced concrete the larger ones might well pass through a mesh of three quarters of an inch. In such a case the smallest might not pass through a mesh of three sixteenth of an inch. Obviously the mix would have to be well graded between these

limits. For very fine aggregate the sand should pass through a three sixteenth mesh but no more than about five per cent of it should go through a mesh having 10,000 holes to the square inch. (Grading sieves are still referred to in Imperial measures.)

Proportions of the constituents of concrete depend in such factors as the kind of work being undertaken, the size of the aggregate being used and the appearance of the concrete when properly set. For excavations which do not require much strength a concrete may consist of some eight to ten parts of fine and coarse aggregate and one part of cement. But for any reinforced concrete work one part of cement, two parts of sand and four parts of gravel may well be needed. Rather obviously the parts are by volume.

Providing enough water is used to promote the chemical reaction of the cement as little of it as possible should be used. The water will eventually evaporate leaving voids in the finished concrete. The water used should be clean; if you cannot drink it do not use it. Dirty water may contain substances which mix badly with the chemicals in the cement. Always keep the mixing platform clean. Measure the ingredients carefully either with gauge boxes or by the wheelbarrow load. They should be mixed until they form one colour, and, of course, while they are dry. In general it is better to use a mixing machine than to attempt to mix by hand. This saves cement and time as well as producing a better product. Use the concrete as soon as it is mixed to prevent it hardening by the evaporation of the mixing water. This is particularly important during sunny conditions or when there is a drying wind.

The concrete should be allowed to cure slowly. Cover it with wet sacks or spray it with water from time to time. This is useful for a period varying between seven and fourteen days. The temperature of newly laid concrete should not be allowed to fall, below 40 degrees F while it is setting. If it does there may be some loss of strength.

Gypsum

Gypsum is a mineral hydrated calcium sulphate used for making plaster of paris; it is also used for cement. Here are a few notes on making gypsum plasters. It is a sedimentary rock which is chemically formed and it consists of calcium sulphate combined with water. When burnt to something like 120 degrees C. seventy five per cent of the water it contains is driven off. It is then ground into plaster of paris which sets rapidly with water. This material is used with lime plaster. Here it accelerates setting times. It is particularly useful for plaster cornices in situ.

There is also retarded gypsum plaster which is used for fibrous plaster work for which plaster of paris sets too quickly. So in this type of plaster the setting is slowed down by adding some retarder such as pulverized glue during its manufacture. In this way it is suitable for plastering walls and for fibrous plaster work.

Lime

Lime is a caustic and highly infusible solid consisting essentially of calcium oxide which is obtained when calcium carbonic is heated strongly. After it has been burnt in a kiln to get rid of the carbon dioxide the chalk or limestone from which it is made turns to quicklime. To make a putty suitable for plastering or a mortar water is added to this quicklime. This is called slaking. The water combines with the quicklime, breaking it up into powder. Then it forms a paste or putty. The mixture becomes very heated and there is a considerable increase in the bulk.

The type of lime depends on the kind of limestone which is used for its manufacture. Limes may be classed as non hydraulic, moderately hydraulic or particularly hydraulic. In fat limes there is a very rapid slaking action accompanied by a great deal of heat which the volume of the material expands considerably. Hydraulic lime slakes rather more slowly, produces less heat and there is less expansion in the material. A plastic putty results if quicklime is slaked too much water.

Limes made from white chalk or pure limestone are said to be fat limes. This can be obtained in either lumps which can be slaked to form lumps or as a ready made slaked powder, a dry hydrate. The lumps are perhaps less popular today because, if these are used, there has to be a waiting period of some three weeks or more before the material can be used. In contrast the ready slaked powder or dry hydrate can be used immediately by adding water. However this lime can be made into a putty and allowed to stand for some twenty four hours before use if this is convenient. Fat limes set very slowly partly because they may absorb carbon dioxide from the air and partly because they may form silicate of lime which is a very slow job. Fat limes do not set under water.

Hydraulic limes are made from chalk and limestone which contains clay impurities. Here the setting action is due, in part, from absorbing carbon dioxide from the air, and, also in part, from the various chemical reactions between the lime and clay constituents formed during the burning process and the water used for mixing. Consequently such limes attain a certain strength under water and the higher the proportion of clay the stronger they will become. Greystone limes up to twenty per cent of clay and limes which are really hydraulic may have up to thirty per cent of clay and — probably — blue lias limestone. These are rather like Portland cement but they are burnt at a lower temperature and they do not have the strength of the cement. The lias limestone plaster is likely to set hard within a week or so.

Lime plasters

For lime plastering fat or fairly hydraulic limes are generally used. The plaster is usually applied so that it builds up to some three quarters of an inch thick in three layers. The first coat is for rendering and picking up and consists of fairly coarse stuff, usually a mix of greystone lime, sand and water. The proportions are usually of greystone lime one to two or even three of sand. In any plaster which has to be hacked off and discarded it is quite likely that ox hair or even horse hair may be found. The second coat called the floating coat, is made in much the same way except perhaps that there may be slightly less sand. The third and final coat which is used for setting and skimming contains what is usually called "fine stuff" and consists of fat lime slaked to a slurry and mixed with a little sand and sometimes a little plaster of paris. In lime plasters the sand helps to bulk out the total material. It also reduces shrinkage and consequent cracking and it helps carbon dioxide to penetrate the plaster because it makes the layer more porous. But drying such plasters is obviously slow and some time must be allowed to elapse before decorating. Wall paper, for example, should not be hung until at least six months after applying the plaster.

Today gypsum plasters or as they are sometimes called "hard wall" plasters are used for most interior walls where plaster board is not employed. Incidently a skimming of plaster is sometimes used on plasterboard so that the latter looks just like an ordinary plastered room. In very general terms gypsum plaster belongs to one of two groups, plaster of paris type or hard burnt Keens's type.

It should be pointed out that some types of gypsum plaster may be inclined to corrode steel so such plasters should not be used as undercoats for steel mesh or steel slats. Nor is expanded wire lathing really suitable. In such cases use a different plaster for the first coat. Keene's plaster is used quite often for quoins, angles and difficult places in much plastering work.

Stone

In Britain the most important building stones are limestone and sandstone, granite, marble and slate. Limestones and sandstones are sedimentary stones, granites are igneous stones and marble and slate are metamorphic stones. The following notes give some information about the stones and indicate where they have been found. Sadly today some of the quarries are no longer working and the reader seeking a particular stone may have some difficulty in locating a supply.

Britain has a variety of limestone of which oolitic is one particular type. Oolitic stones include Ancaster which is found in Lincolnshire; cream to brown in colour it is suitable for general building. Another stone is the beer stone which is described as chalky; this is very nearly white and comes from Devon. It is fairly soft and is used for carvings in churches and other similar interiors. Ketton is an oolitic stone found in what was once Rutland; it is yellow to cream in colour and is useful for general building. Portland stone is also oolitic; it comes from Dorset and is white to light grey. This Whitbed stone is quite strong and it is durable. It is used for many building purposes. Some other Portland stones are more soft and these are usually employed for interior work. There are various types of Bath stone which are oolitic and which are naturally found at Bath and its district. These stones range from cream to lightish brown; they weather fairly well and carve easily. They are used for both interior and exterior work. Chilmark stone in Wiltshire is an oolitic which is buff to yellow or brown; It is a stone used for most general purposes. Ham Hill stone is also Shelly oolitic; it comes from Somerset and is a lightish brown.

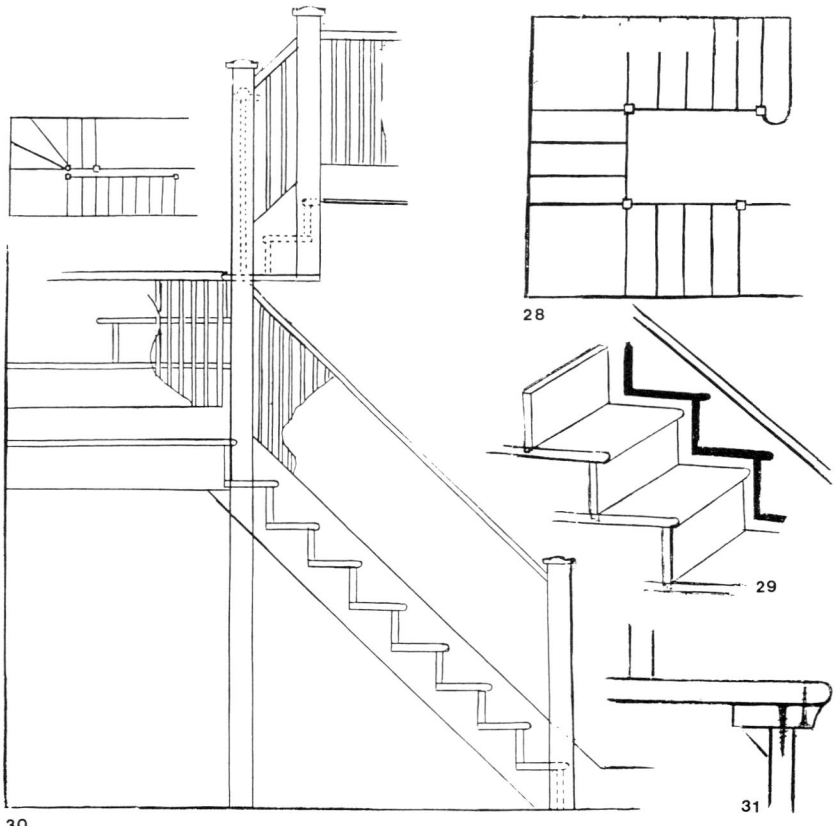

28   Plan view of staircase with two quarter landings.
29   Staircase with treads and risers waiting to be recessed into string.
30   Close newel staircase with a small plan view.
31   A way of fastening treads to risers.

The Dolomitic stones include the following: Anston which is cream and comes from Yorkshire; Bolsover Moor which comes from Derbyshire is cream to brown; Mansfield Woodhouse from Nottinghamshire and is yellow. Purbeck "Marble" which comes from Dorset is a greyish brown Shelly stone.

The sandstones likely to be used in older buildings which may need repairing include the following: Howley, Robin Hood and Bramley Fall all of which come from Yorkshire. The first mentioned and the last mentioned are light brown in colour and both are used for general purposes. The Robin Hood stone is a light grey green and many streets are paved with it. Gloucestershire has two popular stones, the Forest of Dean stone and the Pennant, the first of these being a greyish light blue and the second a greenish slate. The Pennant was often used for paving. Gorsehill stone came from Dumfries and was pink and dark red; besides being used for general work it was also popular for carvings. Craigleith stone came from around Edinburgh and was white or grey or blue; some may still be around today as the stone is extremely durable and was used for many purposes. It should be noted that what is referred to as York Stone may well be one of several sandstones. The granites include the following; from Aberdeen there is the Correnie and the Rubisla. The first of these is a pinkish red and the second is grey. At Aberdeen there is also the Peterhead which is a coarse grained red stone; Creetown comes from around Kirkcudbright-shire and is a light grey. Shap comes from Westmorland and is a reddish colour.

Metamorphic stones are stones which have changed over various periods of time. Mostly they are either sedimentary or igneous and they have been changed by pressure and heat or sometimes by both. Slate, for example, have come about because of the pressure in clays and shales while marbles are limestones which have altered through much the same causes.

Marbles are still employed extensively for interior work and monuments. They are of a compact crystaline make-up and they can be obtained in a variety of colours from different parts of the world. Their veinings are an important part of their charm. There are quarries in France, Belgium and Greece while the famous Carrara marble comes from Italy. There is a little marble in Anglesey, Ireland and Devon.

Roofing slates have been metamorphosing for millions of years and the great pressure from the middle of the Earth has changed the clays and shales from which they started. The pressures produced cleavages planes which formed obliquely in relation to the original sedimentary planes. The rocks then split into slates but these were not necessarily parallel to the original beds. At one time the best slates came from quarries in Bangor, Llanberis and Blaenau Festiniog in North Wales. The slates — which are very scarce today — are a blue, purple in colour. The other centre was Cornwall (Delabole) which produced grey, blue-green and brown slates. The Lake District, Somerset and parts of Scotland have, at times, also produced good building slates.

Apart from natural defects in the stones and the effects of the

32-38   Different doors. Note the gossip door in 38.

atmosphere expansion due to frost and the actions of salts all tend to make stonework on buildings decay. This applies to cathedrals and other buildings down the scale. Vents open up after a time with the action of the weather. Sometimes this is not particularly harmful but it spoils things when the purpose of these is ornamental. It is also true that open vents encourage moisture and dirt and ultimately contribute to the stone decaying. Some stones have soft spots in them due to the fact that when they formed, there was an extra amount of clay which did not harden quite like the rest of the stone. Bad craftsmanship may also be the cause of breakdown. Stone may be used with its natural bed in the wrong position. Pollution of the air is another cause. Limestones, for example, react badly to smoke laden conditions. Sulphur gases dissolve in rainwater and this produces a weak acid which reacts with the calcuim carbonate in the stone. The surface becomes blackish and becomes detached. The iron cramps used in some stonework also rust in due course. This contributes to decay. Cramps of alloy steels are much better or nickel, copper or bronze. Sandstones and limestones should not be used together in the same building. The chemicals which form in the limestone because of polluted rain get into the sandstone and help to produce conditions which encourage decay. When repairing old stone buildings do not use too strong a mortar.

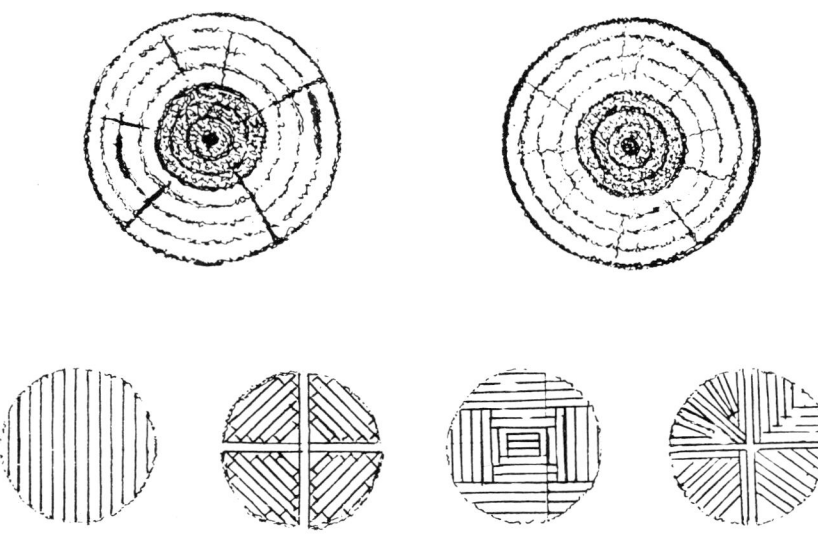

39 Converting lumber to timber.
    Six ways to do it.

Bricks

Many bricks are needed for the repair and maintenance of buildings.

Clay, the traditional material for brick making, is still used very considerably. Today more calcium silicate bricks are also being produced. One of the uses of these bricks is for flexible paving. The new pedestrian precincts to be found in both our new towns and existing ones use a great many calcium silicate bricks.

To be of use for repair bricks must be sound, i.e. free from flaws, cracks and stones. Even small lumps of lime are dangerous for they may slake on exposure to moisture so that the bricks split. On the other hand finely divided lime may be an advantage as it may provide a flux for vitrification. The shape of bricks is obviously important; so is the size for they must build into a wall which is uniform both for appearance and strength. The arrises should be sharp and the angles must be right angles except in special shapes. In general the mortar should be rather weaker than the bricks, otherwise the wall may crack and, eventually, break up. Colour and texture are obviously important and, when repairing existing brickwork, should match existing brickwork as closely as possible. The texture must be uniform throughout the batch. Bricks are produced with various textures such as rough or fine smooth, glazed or sand faced. Some bricks are mottled. When building (or repairing) arches or when undertaking ornamental work cutting and rubbing brick may be needed, for such purposes bricks must be of uniform texture and properly baked. For refractory bricks there must be high infusability to make them suitable for use in furnaces. Most flettons will absorb some twenty per cent of their weight when they get very wet. In other kinds of brick absorption may vary from about one sixth to about one fifteenth of the weight.

We shall now turn our attention to bricks made from brick earths and some mixture thereof. Later we shall deal with special materials.

Wire cut bricks are those which have been made in a special way rather than with particular material. They are produced in blocks and the machine then cuts them into individual bricks. It follows that wire cut bricks cannot have frogs, i.e. indentations to hold mortar. Many different materials are used for wire cut bricks.

Red rubbers are bricks with a very fine texture which are used for gauged work. They may be of various colours in spite of their name.

Facing bricks are those used for most brick houses — at any rate on the front and outside. They may be fine sanded or coarse sanded and the colours may vary considerably. Some may be mottled but all facing bricks have a better appearance than flettons. There may be light and dark reds, cherry red, silver, grey, dark purple brown, blue purple, oak, moss green etc. There is virtually no end to the colours in which facing bricks may be obtained.

In addition there are engineering bricks which are usually red and very difficult to cut; they have a semi gloss finish due to their burning. They absorb very little water and can withstand considerably pressure.

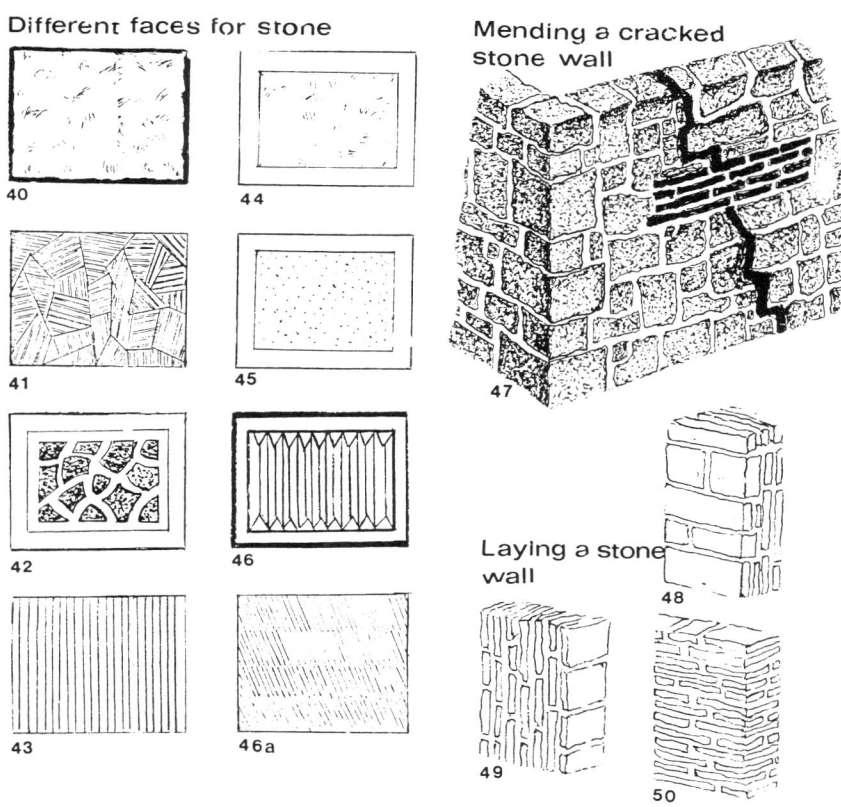

Different faces for stone

40

44

41

45

42

46

43

46a

Mending a cracked stone wall

47

Laying a stone wall

48

49

50

40 Rock face.
41 Dragged.
42 Reticulated.
43 Tooled.
44 Scabbed.
45 Pointed.
46 Furrowed.
46a Boasted
47 Mending a cracked stone wall with brickwork.
48 The wrong way to build a stone wall.
49 Also the wrong way to build a stone wall, although slightly better than the first example.
50 The best way to build a stone wall.

Staffordshire blue bricks may be almost black although they are, technically, blue. Being very vitrified they have a smooth and glossy surface and they are virtually impervious to damp and water. Like engineering bricks they can withstand considerable pressure. There are also white bricks, and Suffolk whites. At one time breeze or clinker bricks were very popular. In many houses built between the two world wars they were inserted into brickwork just where fixings for joinery and woodwork were needed.

Sand lime bricks are made differently. Lime as a binding agent is mixed with sand (about one of lime to ten of sand) and the resulting mix is ground very fine before water is added. The wet material is then boiled in the mixer and stored in silos for a few days for the lime to slake properly. Then they are compressed into bricks and put into a hardening chamber where they are compressed still further. After several hours the bricks are ready for the builders merchant.

Calcium silicate bricks are produced by steam autoclaving. This takes place under pressure. The material is a finely divided mixture of sand and lime and there is a reaction between the surface of the particles of sand and the lime. This produces a calcium silicate hydrate in about twelve hours. Dimensional tolerances compare very favourably with clay bricks as the process does not produce alterations of size. Providing the constituent materials are free of clay and organic impurities there are no soluble salts present or discolouration.

Calcium silicate bricks are not, generally speaking, quite as strong as clay bricks; this means that the mortar must be very slightly weaker to avoid crack developing in walls. In such bricks movements of moisture are rather higher than those of clay bricks and consequently they should not be saturated before being used. Nor should they be wetted before plastering or rendering.

If calcium silicate bricks are used for a stretch of walling which is partly built with clay bricks trouble may occur. Apart from appearances there may be differences in the thermal movements of such a wall and sometimes cracking may occur. While calcium silicate bricks are considered suitable for most purposes their chemical resistance is not always quite as good as that of clay bricks and some slight deterioration may occasionally take place after a period of years in a polluted atmosphere.

The environment in which bricks are used is very important and has a bearing on how they behave. Calcium silicate bricks if laid in wet conditions, may tend to shrink especially when used internally. Thus they may crack particularly if the mortar used is too strong. On the other hand clay bricks may be the subject of irreversible expansion if they are dampened too much and it is certainly bad practice to lay clay bricks which have only very recently come out of the kiln.

It should, of course, be appreciated that brick manufactures like the

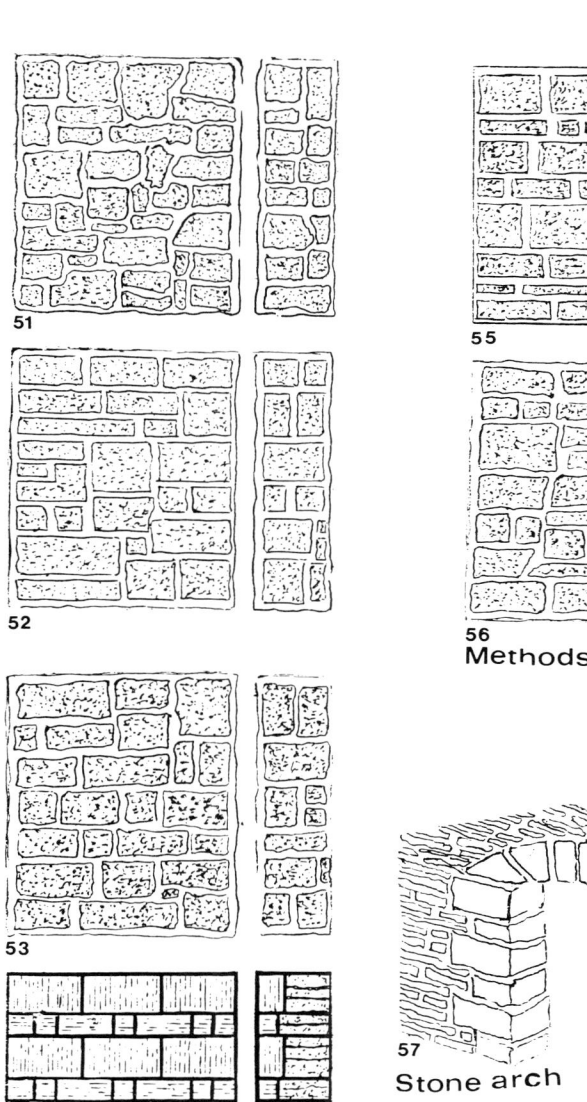

Methods of laying stone

Stone arch

51 Uncoursed random rubble.
52 Squared rubble.
53 Random rubble in course.
54 Squared regular.
55 Squared rubble in course.
56 Square snecked rubble.
57 A stone arch.

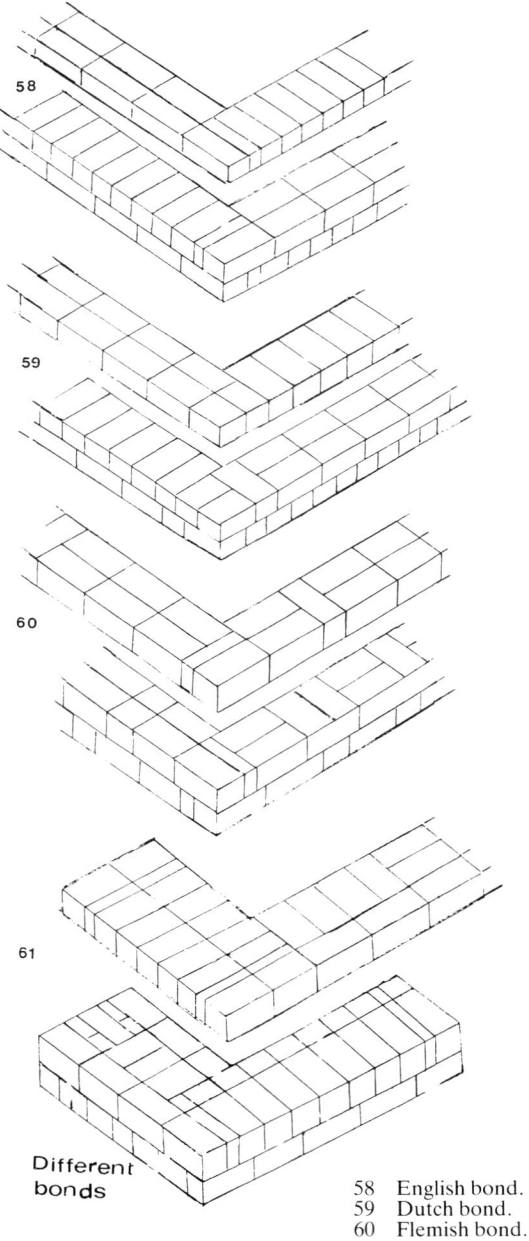

Different bonds

58 English bond.
59 Dutch bond.
60 Flemish bond.
61 2-brick wall in English bond.

makers of other building materials are constantly finding ways of improving their products. The progress which the makers of calcium silicate bricks have made during the last few years has been remarkable.

If the reader is being asked to repair existing brickwork he or she will obviously need to know the dimensions which he or she is likely to have to work to. In the southern counties the length of a brick is double its width plus the thickness of a vertical joint. There should be four courses and four joints to a vertical foot and joints should be ¼ inch thick plus ¹⁄₁₆ to allow for irregularities in the bricks. Thus the length from centres of joints is 9¼ inches. In the north the dimensions are to be the same except that four courses of bricks plus four joints are to be thirteen inches vertically and not twelve.

Roofing Tiles

Roofing tiles come in various shapes and sizes. Plain tiles are nearly flat but they are slightly cambered in their length so that, when laid, they are slightly convex and fit smugly on the tiles below. Various sizes are made particularly 10½ by 6½ inch or 11 by 7 inches are also made. Most of these tiles have a couple of small nibs which stick out below the top edge. These nibs are intended to fit over the battens. In addition each tile has a couple of holes close to the upper edge to take nails. Then there are special shapes intended for verges and abutments to form laps where required.

There are also eaves tiles shaped to avoid cutting and hip and valley tiles for such places. Ridge tiles come in several shapes including half round, winged with a roll, winged with ornamental tops and saddle-back. Finials and intersecting ridge tiles are also available. There are also tiles the lower edges of which are shaped in special forms these are frankly ornamental tiles. It should be appreciated that many of these special tiles are very dated and that builders wanting to find some for a repair job may have to search different merchants to do so. Interlocking tiles come in various shapes and they are generally rectangular in shape; their surfaces are corrugated to enable them to fit the next tile. Pantiles are shaped rather like a flattish S, with a stub projecting from the back. This projection is usually near the upper edge and its purpose is to allow the tile to be fixed to the tile battening.

The making of roof tiles is rather similar to the making of bricks, except that, for roof tiles, the clay has to be much finer because tiles, in section, are thinner than bricks. However the pugging, moulding and burning are very much the same. In years gone by pantiles were first made flat and then curved over. Today there may be some difficulty in obtaining just the right kind of pantile needed for a repair. It should also be remembered that many tiles are now made of conrete. The old hand made tiles were usually of excellent quality; If they now need attention it is likely that the nails fastening them have corroded or the tile battens have decayed. Bedding tiles in mortar is to be avoided as far as possible because the mortar is inclined to hold water from rain and the tiles may become broken due to frost etc. The roofs pitch may be too flat, especially at the eaves where there are sprockets because of the water which is likely to encourage water on the surface.

Gauge between nails should not be more than 4 inches giving a lap

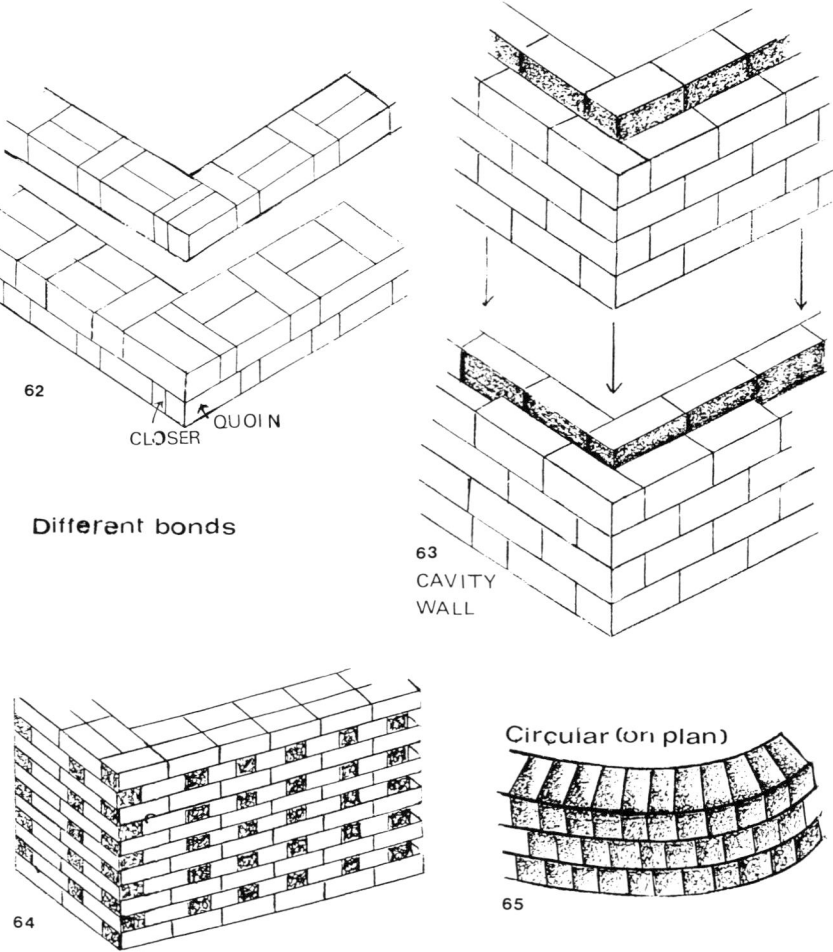

62   An example of Double Flemish Bond showing a closer and quoin.
63   An ordinary cavity wall such as most houses are built of today.
64   An example of Flemish garden bond.
65   A wall built in a circle when considered on plan.

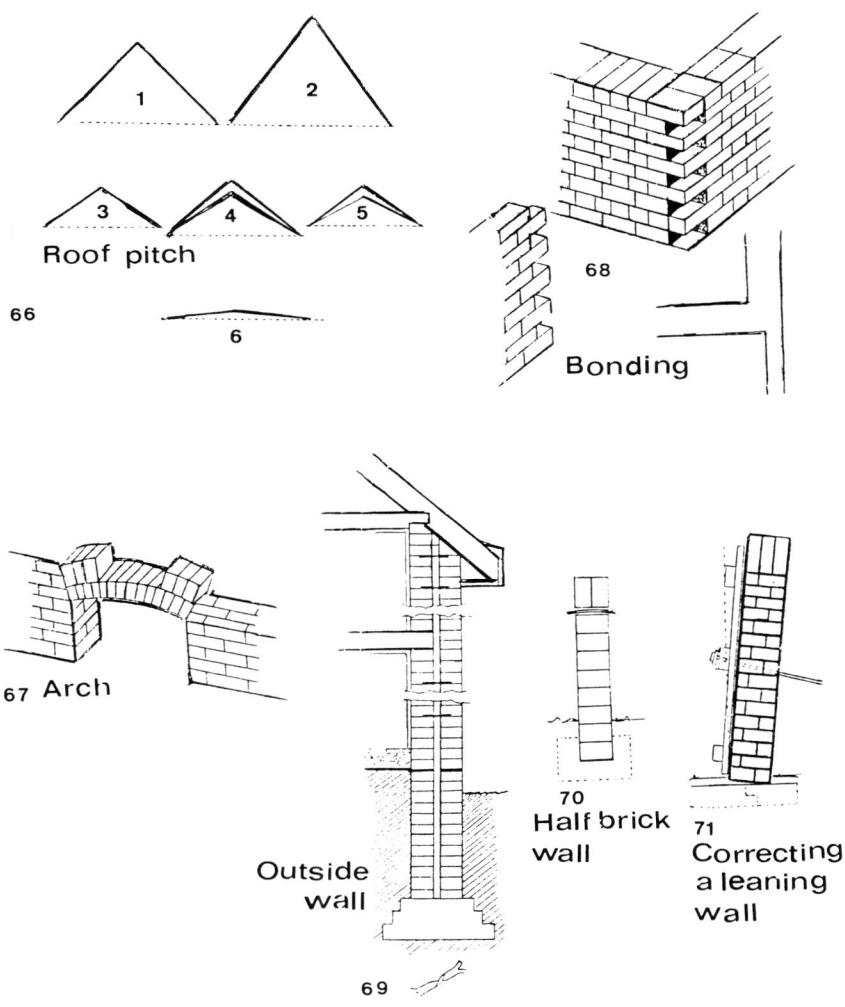

Roof pitch

66

Bonding

68

67 Arch

Outside wall

70 Half brick wall

71 Correcting a leaning wall

69

66 1 For tiles. 2 For thatch. 3 For single lap tiles. 4 For single lap tiles or slates. 5 Small or ordinary slates. 6 So called flat roofs.
67 A brick arch in the making.
68 Bonding a one brick wall to a half brick wall.
69 An outside wall (cavity type). This consists of two half brick walls. Note the stay used to join the two walls every four courses.
70 A half-brick wall.
71 An attempt to correct a leaning wall. First place a vertical where the dotted line is shown and put a bolt through the wall. Then excavate half the width of the wall and pull it upright with the bolt being tightened. Then excavate the other half of the wall and make good with concrete. This is a very delicate operation.

between 10½ inch tiles of 2½ inches. In some cases 3¾ inch gauge is used which gives greater protection against driving rain. In general terms it is desirable to have a good lap if the pitch is inclined to be flat. Camber to the tiles is important; there should be approximately a ¼ inch camber in the lengthways of the tile. The tiles may be fixed to battens only, to battens and felt or to counter battens and battens. But the best way is to close board the roof and to use a good felt over it. Tiles without nibs are then used; these are nailed on the top of the felt. This keeps out the cold and damp. For work of the best class the roof is close boarded and has counter battens some 2 inches by 1 inch thick nailed over the centre line of the rafters. The tile battens are then fixed across these and the tiles are then hung by their nibs to the laths. This provides insulation by creating a space under the tiles. To keep the bond in course half tiles and one and a half tiles are available. These are used at the start of alternative courses. Of the two, the one and a half tile is probably the better because it provides a better fixing.

When a tile is laid the underside is called the bed and the upper side is the back. The lower edge is the tail and the upper edge is the head. The part of a tile exposed to the weather is the margin while the gauge is from nail hole to nail hole. The lap is the degree to which a tile covers the next but one beneath it. Special tiles are made for the eaves and the ridge; the width of these is that of ordinary tiles but the under eaves tiles is 7 inches long and the under ridge tile is 9 inches long. A half tile measures three and three quarters of an inch wide and tile and a half measure nine and three quarters of an inch wide.

Hip and valley tiles are shaped to fit the hips and valleys of a roof. The pitch of the valley should not become too flat. A roof pitch of 40 degrees gives a valley 31 degrees. Valley tiles are either angular or rounded. When repairing old houses the need for a mitred valley tile may be required to replace one which has broken. Such tiles are not greatly used today and the reader will need to search his or her builders merchant. Laced and swept valleys are not easy to make water tight. They take longer to do and so are more costly. A great many tiles have to be cut, but they look quite well when laid.

If a laced valley has to be built a tile and a half requires to be placed across the valley; its point should be below the tiles in that course. Then lay a wide board along the valley to flatten the angle and let the battens finish against this. When these tiles are laid they will have an upward sweep.

Obviously the nails to be used are important. If possible the reader should try to obtain the same kind of nails as were used in the roof before it needed repairing. It is not always possible or economical to do this and substitute nails may have to be used. The best nails for roofs are of zinc composition and copper. But today many galvanized nails are often employed. Zinc nails were often used in days gone by but they could not always withstand sea air. So they were unpopular near the coast. If the reader is repairing some municipal building or other important structure he or she may well find copper nails. It may be possible to replace these with composition of an alloy of copper, zinc and tin if these can be obtained as replacements. They are easier to drive home.

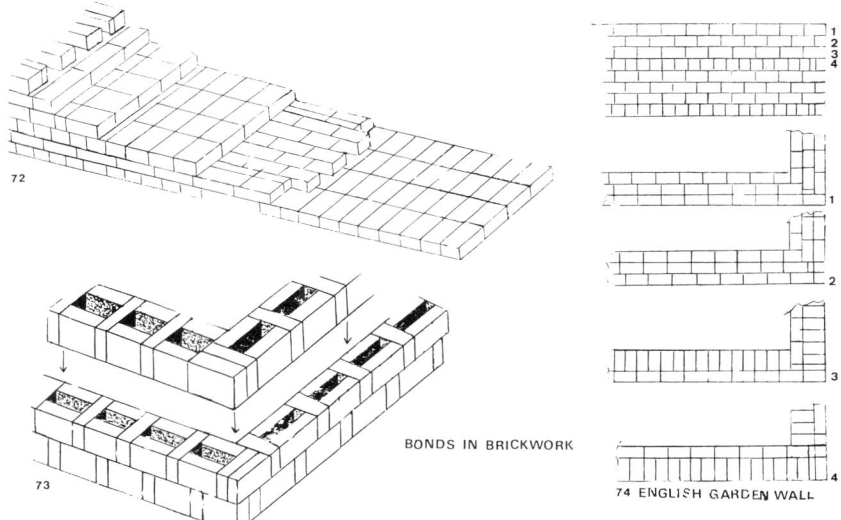

BONDS IN BRICKWORK

74 ENGLISH GARDEN WALL

72   A 4-brick wall with stretchers in the interior for longitudinal strength.
73   Rat trap bond. The alternative courses vary.
74   English garden wall bond. When this is used it should be matched up when repairs are carried out.

Metals

Metals of one kind or another play an extensive role in restoring old buildings. In some cases it is not so much a matter of replacing a metal but rather of using it to improve whatever has to be attended to. A metal may prove to be the best and most economical way of achieving the desired result. Metals have properties not found in other groups of materials. They have considerable tensile and compression strength and they can deform plastically without damage. Sometimes metals are used in buildings as alloys. These consist of an intimate mixture of metals and even, in some cases, of non metals. Metal fatigue means a reduction in strength due to prolonged variations in loading; usually fatigue damage starts as a fault in the metal.

Like other materials metals sometimes fail. For example electrolytic corrosion may occur in brass plumbing fittings in certain kinds of water. This may cause zinc dezincifucation. The remedy is to use low zinc content brass gunmetal. Where there are traces of copper deposited in the flow of water which may happen galvanised water cisterns are used with copper pipes. Here the galvanised film may corrode electrolytically at any point of contact with the copper. The film is destroyed and the steel corrodes. The remedy here is to use a sacrificial anode in the cistern or have a plastic or copper cistern. In some cases iron or steel railings set in stone plinths using lead may be giving trouble. Here the metal should have been protected by several good coats of paint. Sometimes steel radiators with copper pipes and cast iron boilers may corrode. Such corrosion may usually be reduced by using inhibitors.

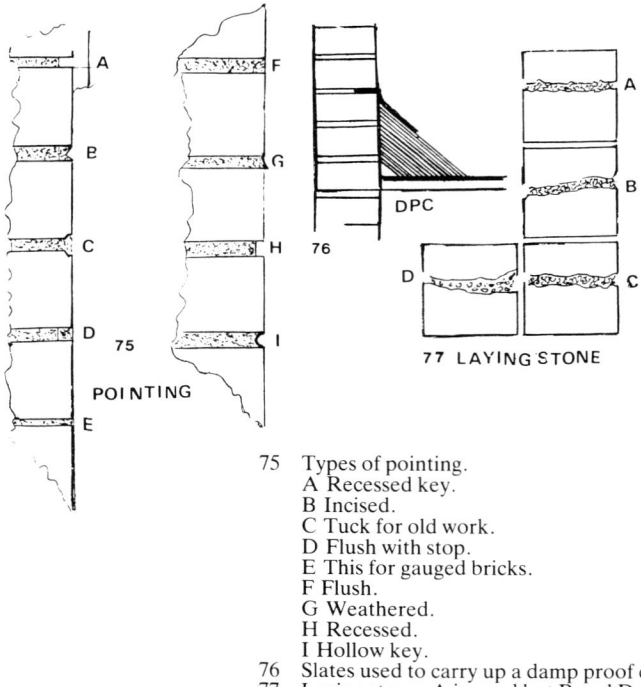

75 Types of pointing.
A Recessed key.
B Incised.
C Tuck for old work.
D Flush with stop.
E This for gauged bricks.
F Flush.
G Weathered.
H Recessed.
I Hollow key.
76 Slates used to carry up a damp proof course.
77 Laying stone. A is good but B and D are not so good.

Iron

Iron is an element which is almost as common as aluminium. When extracted from its ore it can be used in many different ways. When it is in the form of ore it is usually iron oxide together — most probably with some silica and alumina. In the blast furnace the iron oxide is reduced to iron by carbon monoxide which is made by the ignnition of coal and limestone so that the combustible gases provide the heat required.

Slag forms on top of the liquid iron. This slag consists of the impurities and calcium oxide. The iron is run into mounds called 'pigs' which also contain carbon, sulphur, silicon, phosphorus and manganese. This is how wrought iron starts; it has a very low carbon content. Steels also start in the same way; these may have a low carbon content, a medium one or a high one. Cast iron on the other hand has a high carbon content. These materials may be used in the form of alloys in some cases. Wrought iron is the purest kind of iron. Steel is really an alloy of iron and carbon; steel may be considered as embracing many different grades; there are low carbon steels, mild steels, medium carbon steels and high carbon steels. For structural use steel may be hot or cold rolled and bars or wire for pre stressed concrete and for reinforcements are available. In general there may not be a great deal of call for steel in repairing old houses, but, on occasion, there may well be a need for a rolled steel joist to replace an old timber.

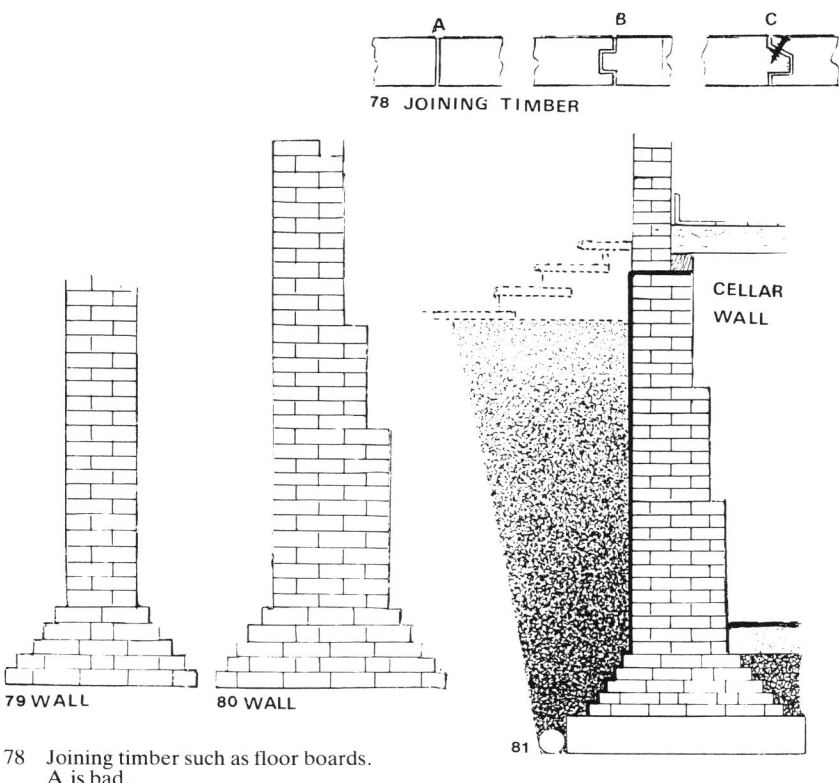

78 JOINING TIMBER

CELLAR WALL

79 WALL   80 WALL   81

78   Joining timber such as floor boards.
       A is bad.
       B and C are much better.
79   Wall showing good foundations. This is a one and a half brick wall.
80   Graduated wall (one and a half bricks thick, two bricks thick and two and a half bricks thick with foundations spreading to five bricks thick.
81   One way to treat the wall of a damp cellar. Dig out as indicated and insert damp proof course right up to the first floor as shown. Fill in the excavation with rubble or stone laying a drain pipe at bottom.

Steel

Alloy steels contain a good deal of alloying elements. Alloys are used to increase the hardness and strength of steel and improve the resistance to corrosion. In some cases alloys impart special properties to steel. Stainless steel, for example, includes chromium; some stainless steels have 18 per cent of chromium and others even more. Most stainless steel is made in the form of steel plate, strip or sheet.

Cast iron is really a carbon and iron alloy. Several different forms of cast iron exist and they get their differences from the condition of the carbon in the metal. The fact that each is extremely castable really unites them. Because of their high carbon content some of them have a very low melting point. There is, for example, spheroidal cast iron, grey cast iron and white cast iron.

We shall now turn our attention to non-ferrous metals.

Non ferrous metals

Aluminium

Aluminium is the most common metallic element in the crust of the earth. It is usually present in most clays and rocks. However to extract it is very expensive and today the principal mineral used for extracting it is bauxite. Pure aluminium is suitable for foils and weathering. But its strength is not great. It is not desirable to allow aluminium to come into physical contact with paints containing copper, lead, graphite and mercury. These should be avoided but the resin based primers with chromates and iron oxide are not harmful. On flooring magnesium oxychloride should be avoided. If allowed to contact aluminium it may corrode it. Aluminium alloys may have better strength and be less likely to corrode. Strength is increased by silicon or copper due to age hardening and sometimes by precipitation.

One great advantage of aluminium is its low density when compared with that of steel. Furthermore in non polluted atmospheres aluminium may be left unpainted. Welding aluminium has proved difficult in the past. Before this can be undertaken the film of oxide must be removed. This can be done by electric arc welding in an inert atmosphere such as argon which excludes oxygen.

Copper

Copper occurs naturally in ores together with iron and sulphur. A great deal is also recovered from scrap and reprocessed. After the impurities are removed by oxidation in a converter or by flotation the metal is then refined by a furnace or electronically; the process chosen depends on the use to which the refined copper is to be put. Except for staining copper behaves like a cathode to other metals used in building. It is protected by virtually every other metal it touches but this happens at the risk of the

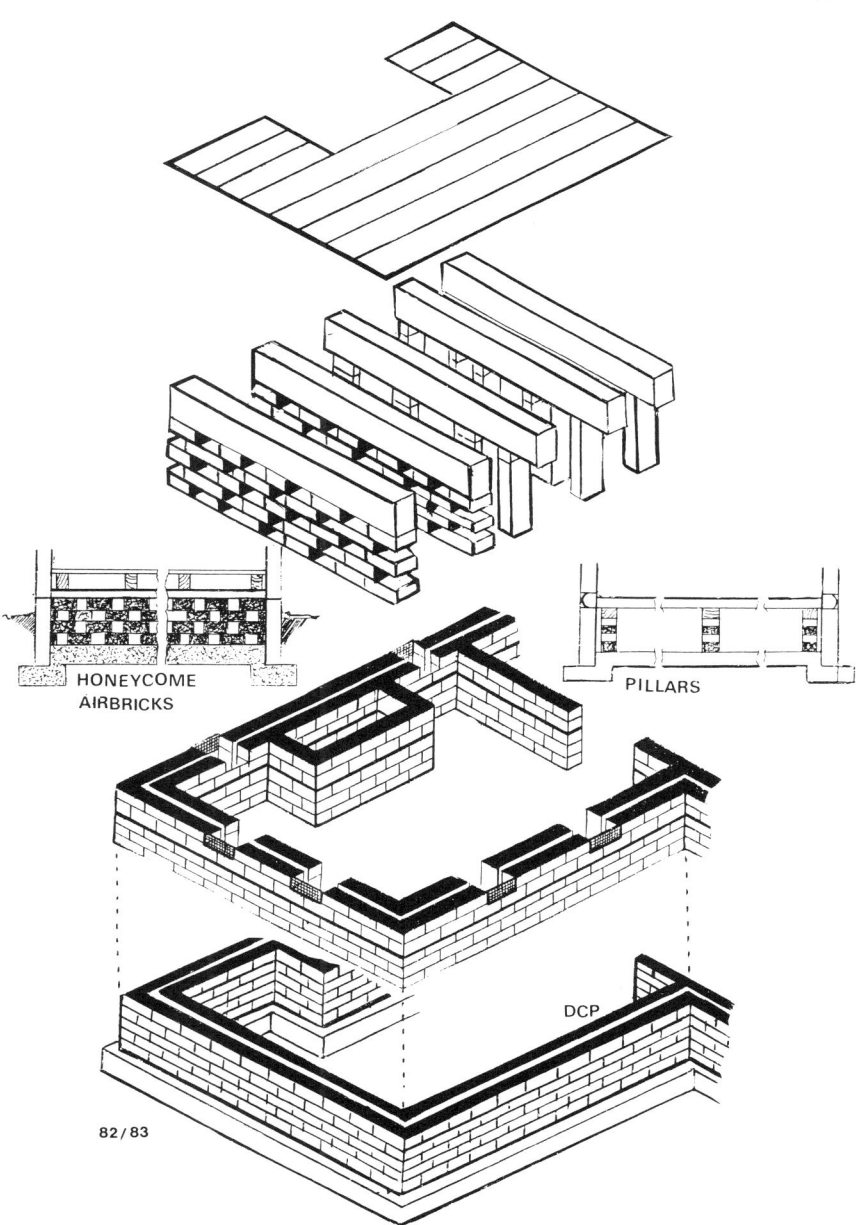

HONEYCOME AIRBRICKS

PILLARS

DCP

82/83

Setting out the footings and showing the damp proof course. Also showing two methods of ventilating under the floor: one by using honeycombe air bricks and the other with pillars.

other metals. The tensile strength of copper depends on its purity. It is very ductile and it has high thermal and electrical conductivity. At normal temperature there is no creep. Perhaps the most useful alloy of copper is brass. Zinc is used to obtain alpha beta brasses suitable for high temperature work.

Lead

Lead is very easy to work and it is extremely durable. Hence its very wide use for weathering matters such as flashings. Years ago it was also used for pipes but plastic is now taking over that job to a very large extent. Lead is also expensive when compared with other materials. Also lower ductility of some other metals makes components very suitable for machine forming. Lead sulphide in the form of galena is imported from America, Canada and Australia, extraction is by converting lead sulphide, to lead oxide. This is then reduced using carbon to the metal as we know it.

Lead has a low melting point and high thermal movement. Strength is low. When exposed to the atmosphere lead forms a coating of lead carbonate which protects it and which does not stain brickwork. It may sometimes undergo electrolytic corrosion with copper and other metals if these come into intimate contact with each other in damp weather. This corrosion is likely to be more serious if relatively large areas contact each other. Small patches of contact are unlikely to be particularly serious. For example lead in sheet form may be secured by copper nails and very little harm will be done. Incidentally, it should be made clear that steel or galvanised nails are not suitable for this purpose.

Lead is really unsuitable for domestic waste systems since, in soft water areas, it may be attacked by certain organic acids, particularly acetic acid. There may also be some corrosion if certain woods such as teak, or oak or even peat are allowed to be in intimate contact if they get damp. If possible lead should be protected with bitumen impregnated tape.

Many old houses and buildings have lead pipes and these may need renewing. Wherever possible plastic should be substituted. This is quite satisfactory for cold water applications and plastics are now beginning to be available which will also withstand hot water as well. For gas supplies extruded lead pipes and, indeed, meter connections are still widely used because of their resistance to corrosion and because of their ductility. However service pipes for water are today increasingly in plastic. In the case of very pure water supplies or rather soft ones these sometimes dissolve lead. This is because the carbon dioxide such water contains sometimes combines with the metal and forms soluble lead carbonate. On the other hand in hard water districts containing calcium carbonate pipes soon become protected by a lead carbonate film which forms on them preventing the dissolution of the metal.

Local authorities may restrict the use of lead contents of mains water and the soft water may require special treatment to keep contamination by lead to certain limits.

Because lead pipes are flexible they can withstand the action of frost with water inside them and they are likely to be able to do this several times. However leaks may develop around the junctions in underground lead pipes because of this reason.

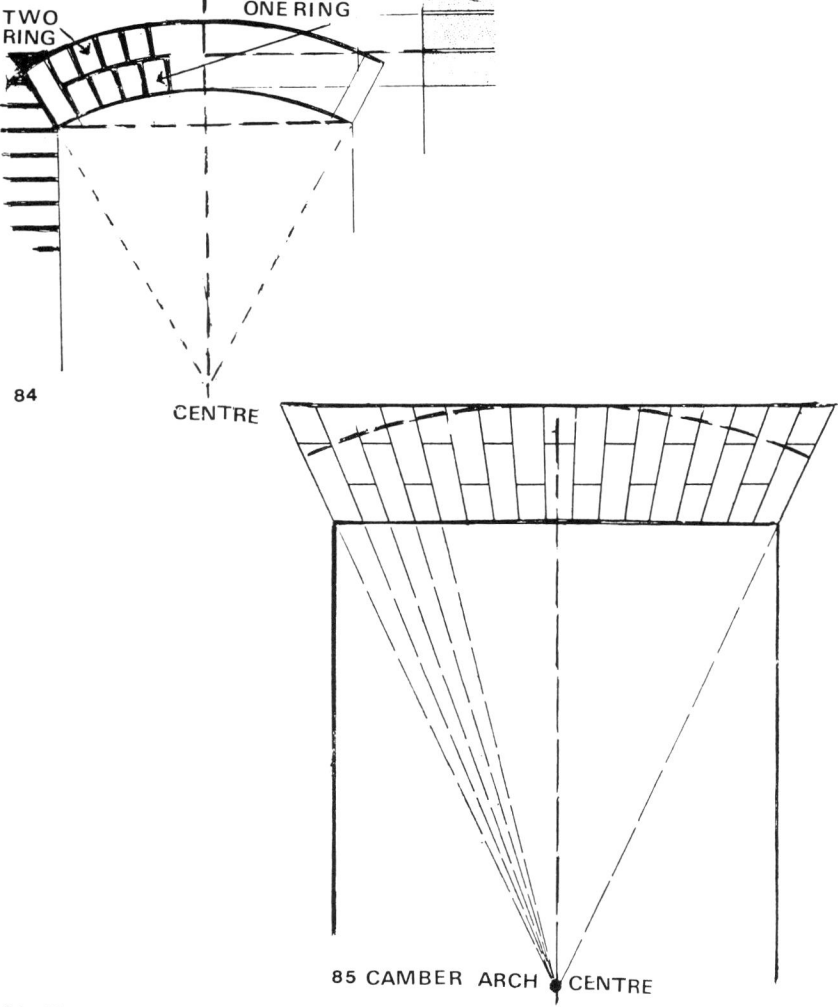

84　How to set out a two ring centre arch.
85　How to set out an arch with a camber centre.

Lead sheet and lead strip are still used in prestigious buildings rather than for private houses. For domestic property lead has largely been replaced by other materials. However there are still many examples of lead roofing, fascias and cladding which are very durable and look extremely attractive. In large areas joints need to be provided to allow for thermal expansion. In any one direction no area should be larger than three metres. In most cases the sheets are used in strips of about a metre wide. Lead strips are still used in damp proof courses although they now compete with bituminous materials.

Lead solder consists of lead and tin with a small amount of antimony. When a low melting point is needed such as for spigot type joints on lead pipes an expensive type of lead solder is needed with a good deal of tin in it.

Bronze
Bronze is an alloy of copper and tin. Most bronze is stronger and harder than brass. It is very durable and is still in demand for ornamental work. In some applications where brass might corrode bronze is used instead of brass. Incidentally British copper coins were, for years, 95.1/2 bronze, 3 per cent tin and the rest zinc. In building bronze is occasionally used for decorative elements in buildings.

Glass
The raw materials of glass are cheap and plentiful and the properties of light transmission, resistance to weathering and abrasion are first class. The most important constituent of glass is silica but this has a very high melting point. So sodium carbonate is added. On heating this forms sodium oxide. However this material is soluble in water so calcium carbonate is added to stabilise it.

Tiny amounts of other materials may also be used, notably borax to produce borosilicate glass which has a low thermal expansion or manganese dioxide which eliminates colour due to colour present in the sand. To make glass cullet or scrap glass is used with the raw materials mentioned and these are heated to some 1500°C. This fuses the materials together and a chemical reaction takes place. The mixture becomes liquid and is allowed to cool to some 1200°C or slightly lower. The molten glass is then ready for forming.

There are four major processes of making glass and these are as follows:
(1) The flat drawn process. Here glass is drawn upwards and it is taken onto a metal grille which is called a bait. Rollers engage the sheet and thereby prevent it waisting. To relieve cooling pressures the glass is then annealed. After this it is cut into sheets. This glass is used in houses and offices.
(2) Rolled glass. Here the molten glass is taken on a horizontal ribbon by rollers and is then annealed. Although this kind of glass does not give a

clear vision it can be used for patterned glass. In some cases wire is incorporated when it is known as Georgian glass.

(3) Float glass. From an optical point of view this is flat. It is made by drawing the glass along on a bath of molten tin. It is greatly valued and is used for such applications as shop windows, mirrors etc. Where undistorted vision is needed.

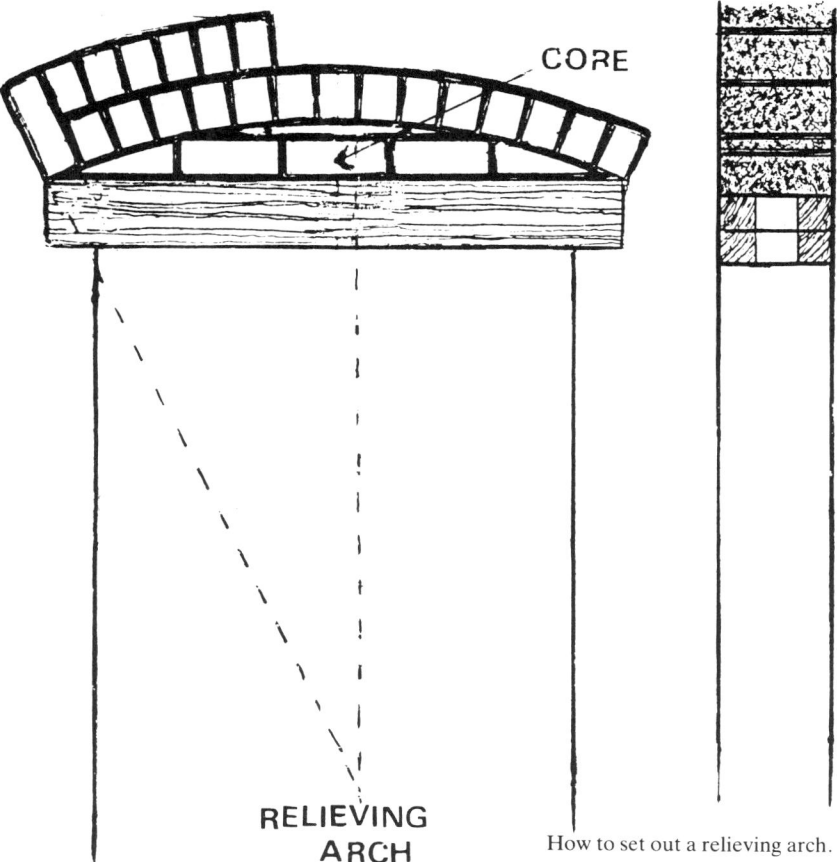

CORE

RELIEVING ARCH

How to set out a relieving arch.

(4) Toughened glass. The strength of most glass is limited by a number of surface cracks but with toughened glass these flaws can be removed by heat treatment. Sheets of glass are heated all over until they just about become plastic and then these are cooled by jets of air so that the outer layers contract and then solidify while the inner layers endeavour to do the same; they produce compression on the outer layers. This closes the microscopic cracks. Thus the impact strength of the glass is greatly

increased. It takes a lot to break toughened glass but when it does go it shatters. In the building trade the applications of toughened glass include doors, large windows and large curtain walls which should be suspended from a structural frame as, in this way, the weight of the glass helps its stability.

Toughened glass cannot be cut; it has to be made to the size required. The thickness of ordinary glass is usually 3 and 4mm but other thicknesses are available. The thickness chosen should increase with the area and wind resistance. Square sheets should perhaps be thicker than rectangular sheets. The thickness of toughened glass depends on the impact it is likely to have to withstand. Single sheet glass relies on the heat loss due to the resistance to its surface. The resistance to heat loss for double glazing depends on the resistance of the four surfaces which double glazing presents.

The thermal movement of glass depends on its composition as well as the thickness. High silica glass such as borosilicates is usually more resistant to thermal shock than lead crystal. Thermal movements sometimes produce movements in glass. In this respect it would be better not to allow glazing tacks to press against the edge of the glass. In the case of suspended glass the sheets may expand down the length of the glass and consequently a flexible joint should perhaps be supplied at the bottom, especially in the case of very large areas. It is also best to have a flexible joint in windows in doors and wherever there is likely to be much shaking. Alkalis such as those which occur in chemical paint strippers or cement may attack the surface of glass and harm its ability to transmit light. The same may be the case if cement touches glass. But glass is not affected by most acids except hydroflouric acid.

Thermo plastics

Plastics may be divided into two principle classes: thermo plastic and thermosetting. We shall deal with thermoplastics first. Thermoplastics means those plastic materials which, when reheated, may be reformed into other shapes. One of the most widely used of these is polyethylene which is also fairly cheap. There are two ways of manufacturing polyethylene. One way involves a high pressure process which makes a low density polyethylene and the other is a low pressure process which makes higher density polymer.

Damp proof courses can be made of such plastic and also sheeting membranes, vapour barriers and shelters. However they are not suitable for gas pipes — particularly the low density ones — as they are very permeable to gases. However low density polythene may be used for cold water applications although it is not as rigid as high density material.

Polypropylene is rather like polyethylene but it gets soft at a higher temperature. Manhole covers, waste systems; even hot water pipes and cylinders may be produced from this plastic. It is also used in certain kinds of fibre reinforcement and also string intended for most purposes. Like polythene, polypropylene is just about the only plastic which is less dense than water. Guttering is another application. PVC has an impact strength which varies according to the temperature. The colder it is the more likely it is to fail. The introduction of fillers and plasticisers can impart to PVC special properties and the plastic can be made transparent for roof lights. Corrugated roofs are also possible. Polyvinyl fluoride is suitable as a plastic coating for metals. In its early days there were problems in bonding it to metals but these have now been overcome. Polytetrafluoroethylene is used mainly as a coating, perhaps because it is almost too expensive to use any other way.

There are a few uses for polystyrene in the building industry, particularly for linings connected with refrigeration. Expanded polystyrene is widely used in insulation and for tiles for ceilings. It is also used for roof insulation. But there is a considerable fire hazard because it burns very readily. Acrylonitrilile butadiene styrene is used for rain water goods.

Acrylic plastics make use of acrylic acid. Perspex belongs to this group. The plastic diffuses light very effectively. When a good surface is required scratches may be removed by polishing. Nylon is used for certain goods. It is capable of resisting most organic solvents, alkalis and weak acids but it gets rather brittle if exposed to prolonged sun light. Central heating tubes made of nylon are easy to cut. Polycarbonates weather very well and are used in sheet form by the building trade.

Thermosetting plastics
Thermosetting materials cannot be melted once they are formed and they cannot be made into other things. Some of the early plastics were thermosetting.

Phenolic resins resist heat very well. The extrusion process cannot be carried out with this plastic. But it has proved itself excellent for electrical goods such as plugs and switches. Today laminates provide one of the most important outlets for phenolic resins. They are also used very considerably as adhesive for wood.

Amino resins
The two most important resins in the amino group are urea and melamine formaldehyde. The urea formaldehyde resins permit a wide range of colours because they are a light colour themselves. Otherwise they are rather like the phenol-formaldehyde resins. They also resist moisture rather better and they certainly have greater impact strength. They are used for toilet seats and other moulded articles. Adhesives represent another application.

Epoxide

These complicated resins have good chemical resistance especially to most alkalis and they are excellent adhesives. They are also used in paint, and for glass-reinforcement.

Polyester resins

These resins are often used with glass fibre. In adhesives they have good fire resistance.

Polyurethane

While some of these are thermoplastic others are thermosetting. The resin is also used in the form for cavity wall insulation and for spraying on pipes. Uses not connected with the building trade include sponges and upholstery. Some polyurethanes are used for surface coatings and resilient gaskets in clay pipes.

So much for the most important plastics used by builders. Let us now consider another group of materials, the silicones.

Silicones

Silicones are semi organic compounds which are tetravalent. Depending on the extent to which silicones have undergone polymerisation will depend on their form. They may be liquids, solids or they may be just rubbery. The fluids are stable at various temperatures and they resist dilute acids and alkalis. In the building industry they are chiefly important because they are very water repellent. This is due to their very low surface tension. These resins are used considerably in paints which are heat resisting; sometimes they act in combination with aluminium pigments when they are useful for painting the flues of boilers. They also play an important part in the protective backing of paper for backing self adhesives. This field includes sealing tapes. Silicone is also used for rubbers to make gaskets. In this respect they are better at high and low temperatures.

Rubbers

Elastomers or rubbers include various types of synthetic rubbers such as polysulphide and silicone, styrene butadiene etc. Such products are used in the making of 0 rings for joining pipes and for fillers, mastics and chlorinated paints. Adhesives also make use of certain rubbers.

Bitumens

Bitumen has an extremely complex structure which is based on carbon and hydrogen. Other elements in bitumens include oxygen, sulphur and nitrogen. The state of the material varies considerably; it may be brittle and hard or a thick viscous liquid. The natural home of asphalt in which bitumen occurs is, of course, Trinidad Lake. It is also found in certain kinds of rocks. Synthetic bitumens can be made by distilling oil; here the volatile fractions are removed leaving a residue, the viscosity of which depends on temperature. Certain bitumens are allowed to become hard with the distillation completed so that they subsequently require softening by solvents. Bitumens are resistant to acids and alkalis. They are used extensively for roofing felts which have the bitumen incorporated with mineral or organic fibres.

Asphalts are far more rigid than pure bitumen although they contain bitumen. They are not only more rigid but also have far greater stability and resistance to abrasion. Asphalts which soften when heated are mastic asphalts. There is a limestone content; the bitumen resists acid but the limestone does not. When there is fear of acids being present siliceous aggregates should be used. Other uses for bituminous products include damp proof courses, adhesives, paints and adhesives. Thermoplastic flooring tiles also make use of bitumens.

Paints

Paint has several functions; to safeguard the surface from the atmosphere; to improve light or heat properties; to provide a decorative finish; for special reasons such as, for example, electrically conductive paints or paints for protecting metals. Of recent years paint technology has advanced considerably and synthetic resins have opened up fresh avenues.

Paint has both a vehicle and a pigment. In many cases there are also extenders. The vehicle is concerned with the paint setting properly, its gloss or matt finish and its impermeability. The pigment controls the opacity, strength, colour and covering power. Solvents and driers may also be used in the formula.

Paints harden within a few hours by several means: polymerisation (chemical reaction) or by oxygen in the air; by the coalescence of an emulsion; or by the evaporation of the solvent. The old days of lead, linseed oil and turpentine have long since passed. Today when linseed oil or tung oil is used it is generally modified by alkyd resins. When boiled linseed oil tends to have better qualities than ordinary linseed, especially in relation to hardening. In some cases driers such as lead, manganese or cobalt may be incorporated into the paint. When these are used they can take oxygen into the molecular structure of the paint to help in polymerisation. When oil based paints harden they behave very much as thermosetting plastics; they are not affected by solvents in the oil. Unless a protective coating of white spirits is applied to the can, such paints harden while stored and form a skin.

Alkyd resins have an important role to play in modern paints. These resins are really a mixture of glycerol and phthalic anhydride, the latter being produced from phthalic acid by extracting water molecules. Alkyd resins are coloured white so varnishes and oil based paints may contain synthetic resins and drying oils so that qualities such as the retention of gloss and colour are good. So is the durability. Indeed these properties are far better than would be the case with pure alkyds or pure oil. Long oil vehicles with a high proportion of oil are flexible and tough and are suitable for outdoor work; short oil kinds are used mainly indoors.

Polyurethane paints come in different kinds. The two pack versions of the resins produce the hardest versions. Really these have extremely good properties. But it should be remembered that tolylene disocyanate vapour is dangerous if inhaled.

The rate at which these paints are cured depends very much on temperature. The two-pack paints are a disadvantage for building sites and they require very accurate mixing. In the building trade the air drying polyurethane paints are very extensively used. These are really drying oils which have been modified. Moist-curing polyurethane varnishes react with water and in damp timber they are said to form an impervious film. But such varnishes do not readily dry in damp timber.

Many oil based paints consist of glyserides of organic acids and so they are formed from glycerol. If sodium hydroxide which is an alkali comes in contact with oil based paint film it may revert to glycerol. This is likely to produce sodium salts or "soap". This means a soapy deposit paint containing oil (including polyurethane) is unsuitable for use on alkaline substates like portland cement. If such paints have to be used in such circumstances an alkali resisting primer should be used. This must be applied before the other materials.

Emulsion paint is used extensively in interior decorating. Polyvinyl acetate emulsions may be applied to new plaster or new cement. Such paints are miscible in water. But when dry coalescence of the molecules occurs which produces a film with some resistance to water. Today there are acrylic emulsions which may be used on timber some of which produce a gloss finish. Non-convertible paints offer some advantage; they do not skin in the can and the various coats applied build into each other. However the dried coats of paint do not tolerate organic solvents very well and in this respect they do not equal convertible paints. Cellulose and bituminous paints are two examples of solvent based paints.

Cellulose may be made of nitro-cellulose dissolved in a solvent of, say, acetone. Synthetic resins are added and they produce a gloss finish while plasticisers provide elasticity. Drying is usually very rapid but good ventilation is a must and there is a fire risk. The coating is highly flammable. Cellulose is best sprayed although retarders can be used for brushing versions. Because they are highly flammable and smell badly when being used they tend to be restricted to factories. However cellulose has an excellent finish and resists fungal attack very effectively.

Bituminous coatings are designed for protecting metals out of doors and thick coats provide very good protection. However they do not have good gloss retaining properties. Sometimes the solvents used tend to lift the paint when other coats are applied so that these 'bleed' and so spoil the decorative effect. The use of aluminium primers directly onto bituminous paint is often recommended to prevent this happening. Chlorinated rubber paints have rather similar properties to these paints.

Adhesives

The whole approach to adhesives has been changed by the advent of synthetic resins during recent years. These resins are now being used for many structural purposes which would not have been considered as suitable for adhesives before the synthetics arrived. Today resins are being used for load bearing applications even where there may be moisture or heat and they are proving to be perfectly satisfactory. In many stress-producing situations there is very little key, but the resins are producing satisfactory bonds between the two surfaces concerned.

Adhesives may be divided into three kinds; animal and casein glues; thermo-setting; thermo-plastic.

Animal glues which have been in use for many centuries are made from bones and some skin of animals. These usually come in the form of powder and they are melted down in warm water. The viscosity of the resulting solution will depend on the kind of surfaces to be stuck together. Such glues do not withstand moist or damp conditions very well; when stored they harden but can be melted again by heating. The best application is concerned with woodwork.

Casein glues are rather like animal glues. However they come from skimmed milk; they are really precipitates by the action of acids. They are usually mixed cold. Casein glues are best used in dry situations although formaldehyde is sometimes used for improving their resistance to damp.

Urea-formaldehyde is commonly used for general woodwork such as joinery. The formaldehyde and urea are made to react together but only to a limited extent. While the resin is still liquid the reaction is stopped. The resins are often of the two pack variety — the resin and the hardener. Such glues produce a very strong bond. However urea-formaldehyde resins have very little 'tack'; consequently during the curing process the two surfaces to be stuck must be held together very tightly.

In some cases the resin may be applied to one surface and the hardener to another. If this is done strong bonds can often be produced within ten or so minutes. This type of adhesive is often used for such things as laminated timber, laminates intended as decoration and flush doors etc. When repairing old buildings the glue will harden at room temperature but it can be accelerated by heated presses or strip heating. The latest thing is to use radion-frequency heating which may reduce the curing period to a few seconds. Sometimes hot water will break down a urea formaldehyde joint.

If this happens — and it probably does near a kitchen sink — use a stronger adhesive for the repair.

Although melamine formaldehyde resin adhesives are more expensive than urea formaldehyde they usually come in powder form and they set when heated to 100°C. Mixed with water they produce a colourless liquid. They have very good weather resistance.

Phenol formaldehyde is used extensively for the laminations in plywood. In liquid form they polymerise when heated at over 100 degrees C. Sometimes this adhesive is used in the form of sheets which bond the surfaces when they are warm. Many of the applications require the addition of a hardener. There are also cold colouring adhesives which are generally insoluble in water but they are capable of setting when acid is added to them. The resulting glue is obviously acidic and may well have ph value as little as 1. Too much hardener shortens the pot life of such adhesives. They are also very hard and rather brittle and wood stuck with this adhesive may sometimes crack, especially if much heat has been used in curing. However, resistance to moisture is excellent. Such glues must be correctly mixed and the maker's instructions should be followed carefully.

Resorcinol formaldehyde is water soluble and is made by using resorcinol with formaldehyde. Curing takes place under room temperature conditions or it can be accelerated by the application of moderate heat. Such adhesives are used extensively for laminated timber and they are very durable in all weathers. But the timber itself may need a preservative.

The majority of preservatives do not affect the adhesive. This adhesive is also used for laminating wood products and for laminating to brickwork and concrete. A little moisture does not seem to hurt them. When bonding to uneven surfaces filler may be needed. Resorcinol adhesives are very hard and brittle.

Polyurethane adhesives have the ability to join metal to unvulcanised rubber. They are fairly resistant to the weather. This group includes elasomers, rigid solids, foams as well as adhesives.

Epoxy resins are used for sticking metal, woodwork and several thermo-setting plastics. As the adhesive sets there is very little shrinkage. Most of these resins are used in the form of two packs but some epoxy resins can be used with organic solvents so that setting occurs by the evaporation of the solvents. In such cases the adhesive can be stored as a liquid. Then they can be used as contact adhesives by applying the resin to both surfaces and allowing it to set for some twenty minutes or so. On being pressed together a bond is created immediately and, indeed, care must be exercised to ensure that the objects to be stuck together are lined up properly. Mistakes are fatal. Such adhesives do not withstand wet conditions very well and the solvents used are highly flammable. The two part versions can be employed for load bearing joints. Repairs in wood and metal are also useful applications for such adhesives.

We shall now consider thermoplastic adhesives. These may set by the evaporation of their solvents, by emulsion coalescence or simply by cooling. In very general terms thermoplastic adhesives are not used for much structural work because such bonds tend to be weaker.

Polyvinyl acetate is used extensively by the building industry for it is used for both woodwork and as a bonding agent in some types of concrete. However one of the materials to be joined must be absorbent. PVA adhesive does not require a hardener. The thin glue lines set quickly but gap filling may sometimes be a problem. Joints withstand impact quite well but not necessarily prolonged stress.

Polystyrene adhesives will join PVC or polymethyl methacrylate but the solvents used are highly flammable.

Rubber based adhesives dissolve in a suitable solvent. Neoprene, for example, makes an excellent adhesive for panels in walls, tiles and for coveings. Until they are cured, these adhesives are highly inflammable but they have excellent resistance to small movements.

Bituminous adhesives make excellent bonds with several different materials. They are flexible and quite good at resisting moisture and damp. In some of these adhesives rubber — natural or synthetic — may be included to impart some elasticity and strength. There are several kinds of bituminous adhesives such as those emulsions which are water based. These are frequently used for wood block floors, thermoplastic tiles and even for PVC. Also used for PVC are the solvent types which are also used for laying linoleum. There should be some absorbency in at least one of the materials to be stuck.

There are also several groups of sealing compounds which it will be convenient to discuss here. Some of these are brittle such as mortars made of gypsum, cement or lime. These may crack and should only be used where tiny cracks will be no disadvantage. Such materials are sometimes used for fixing W.C. pans to soil pipes but they are not particularly suitable for this purpose. However their ductility may be improved by adding emulsified polyvinyl acetate.

Preformed fillers which are sometimes used in building construction to accommodate subsequent movement in the building. Among these fillers is expanded polythene which is commonly used for such things as walls, roads and panels. A sealant should be used to exclude moisture.

There are rubber based sealants which can be useful for filling small gaps. These include bituminous mastics or oil based plastics. But a coat of paint should be applied as well or they will set very hard.

In some cases there may be a fire hazard with some sealants until they are cured.

Chapter 5
OTHER BUILDING MATERIAL, FITTINGS, SERVICES AND MATTERS OF INTEREST

So far we have considered wood, cement, concrete, aggregate, sand, gypsum, lime, stone, bricks, tiles, metals, non ferrous metals, copper, lead, bronze, glass, plastics, paints and adhesives. These are all items of major importance to anyone putting old property into good order. But there are many other materials and fittings which are also of interest to such readers. Here we propose to deal with these, or rather with some of them, as briefly as possible.

Acoustic insulation
This is essential for people who are close to main roads, ports, airports, certain kinds of factories and industrial installations and railway sidings. There are various methods of achieving the desired result, but the most common is by double glazing. Some industrial buildings are now built without windows and obviously this provides acoustic insulation of a kind — among several other things.

If it is desired to provide rooms with partitions, there are insulation systems in the form of panels which merit attention. There are also environmental systems which can be supplied by spray but they need also to be resistant to fire and be thermally efficient. Insulation products include glassfibre and mineral products which are applied to walls and which can be big energy savers. This includes timber frame and external cladding walls. The masking of unwanted sound can also be helped by some of the services offered.

Air conditioning

For old houses fans are useful in helping to air condition areas such as the w.c., bathrooms, kitchens and the like. In some cases automatic

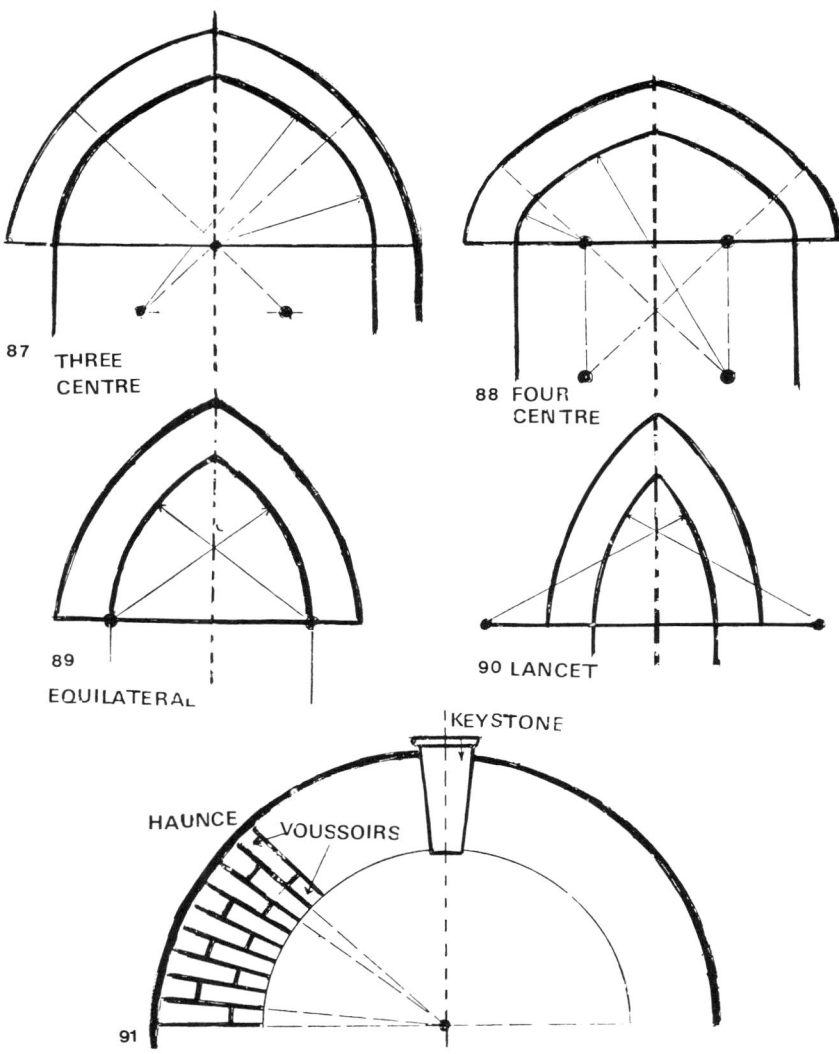

87 THREE CENTRE

88 FOUR CENTRE

89 EQUILATERAL

90 LANCET

KEYSTONE

HAUNCE VOUSSOIRS

91

87 How to set out a three centre arch.
88 How to set out a four centre arch.
89 How to set out an equilateral arch.
90 How to set out a lancet arch.
91 How to set out an arch with a key stone.

condensation control systems are available for bathrooms, w.cs and kitchens. Such units have a built-in sensor to switch the fan on immediately the preset humidity level is exceeded. There are also fans which are automatic and which incorporate automatic sensors and adjustable timing mechanisms.

There are several different kinds of smoke control units and also natural ventilation louvres. In addition there are items which help condensation problems.

Alarms

There is a wide range of burglar and fire alarms available, both for business, industrial and private premises. These range from relatively simple burglar alarms intended for domestic property to security systems for large premises. For fire protection there is the sprinkler system and a range of fire extinguishers.

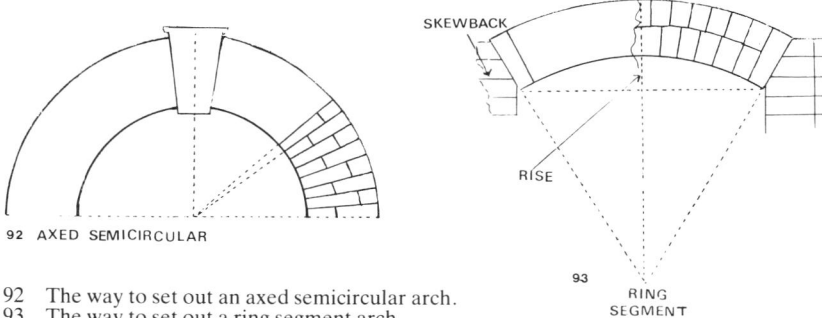

92 AXED SEMICIRCULAR

92   The way to set out an axed semicircular arch.
93   The way to set out a ring segment arch.

Anti-condensation

Many anti condensation fans incorporate powerful centrifugal impellers to permit maximum control units designed for bathrooms, kitchens and similar places. Some units have built in sensors which switch on the fan immediately the pre set humidity is exceeded. In choosing such a unit for domestic purposes remember that a low level of noise is important.

Anti-vandal fittings

Welded wire mesh is used as reinforcement by the construction industry and there is no reason why it should not also be employed for repairing houses which require strong walls or ceilings and floors.

Arch frames

There are solid bead arch frame systems on the market together with gentle curved shapes. For exteriors there are stainless steel arch frames also with solid beads.

Architectural ironmongery

This includes a variety of door and window fittings which are available in different metals and with different finishes and colours. There are also electric door fittings and closing devices. Window fittings also come into this category, some of which have locking devices. There are also cast iron fittings.

ROOF
A cut away picture showing the roof construction. One side tiles and the other slate. Any of the timber members may need renewing in an old house.

Asphalt and mastic

These include roofing felts, paints and tar products. There are cold adhesives, coatings and paints. Some of the roofing materials are made by applying bitumen to fibreglass, polyester, hessian or felt. It is also possible to buy boards surfaced with such materials. Some of these boards are coated with glasscloth.

The following are likely causes of trouble and should be looked at from time to time:

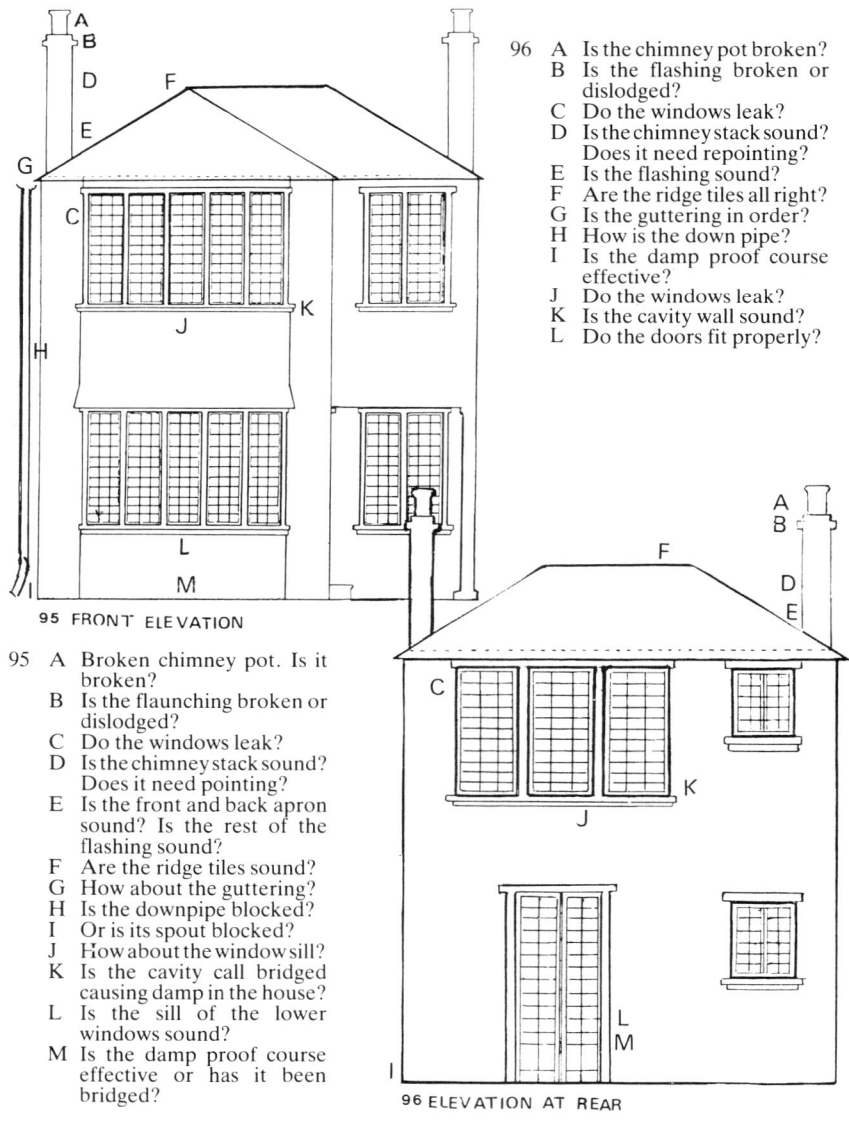

95 FRONT ELEVATION

96 ELEVATION AT REAR

96 A Is the chimney pot broken?
    B Is the flashing broken or dislodged?
    C Do the windows leak?
    D Is the chimney stack sound? Does it need repointing?
    E Is the flashing sound?
    F Are the ridge tiles all right?
    G Is the guttering in order?
    H How is the down pipe?
    I Is the damp proof course effective?
    J Do the windows leak?
    K Is the cavity wall sound?
    L Do the doors fit properly?

95 A Broken chimney pot. Is it broken?
    B Is the flaunching broken or dislodged?
    C Do the windows leak?
    D Is the chimney stack sound? Does it need pointing?
    E Is the front and back apron sound? Is the rest of the flashing sound?
    F Are the ridge tiles sound?
    G How about the guttering?
    H Is the downpipe blocked?
    I Or is its spout blocked?
    J How about the window sill?
    K Is the cavity call bridged causing damp in the house?
    L Is the sill of the lower windows sound?
    M Is the damp proof course effective or has it been bridged?

Bathrooms
Bathroom furniture is today often made of stainless steel or plastic. However there is still some demand for cast iron baths. Ceramics are still popular for wash basins together with w.c. suites. For bedrooms there is the vanity suite. The market for bidets is growing. Usually these are colour co-ordinated with the remainder of the bathroom suite.

Heating
There are many kinds of heating apparatus using a variety of fuels such as gas, electricity, oil and solid fuel. There are also heating systems which rely on heated air being delivered to various parts of the house through louvres, and also underfloor heating. Solar heating is likely to progress during the next few years although today it is still in its infancy.

Ceiling finishes
There are many different finishes some of which are sprayed or applied with a brush or similar tool. Others consist of boards of panels. There are also fibreglass ceilings and a number of suspended ceilings. But the latter are generally used for business premises rather than for homes requiring renovation.

Central vacuum cleaning
This is already popular in America and is beginning to be used in this country. The system consists of a powerful central vacuum unit situated in a garage or out building. This is connected by pipes to various points in the house, the pipes being hidden in the walls. These suction points are located on internal walls so that all areas may be reached by a light weight 8m hose. Obviously it is best to incorporate the system into a house while it is being built, although it should be possible to incorporate the pipes into walls of houses being done up.

Conservatories
Conservatories are available in kit form and some have radius glazed frontages with ventilation and condensation trap systems. Such kits are available in different sizes. Fittings are concealed and give a flush glazed appearance. The box aluminium frame sections are available in electro bonded white or bronze finish.

Excavators
Today hydraulic excavators are often needed for earth moving purposes in connection with property which is being renovated. Unfortunately machines of this kind do not necessarily work well in confined spaces. Consequently compact versions of such machines are of interest to builders doing up old property. Today there are machines which will go through

relatively narrow pathways or doorways and which can easily be manoeuvred. Yet at the same time they can dig astonishingly deep — sometimes down to 2.1 metres with buckets up to 600 metres wide. Both petrol and diesel models are available.

Flashings
The traditional material for flashings was lead and, indeed, it still is. But bituminious products are now appearing and some of these are very good indeed. Lead is still used largely however and it is available in sheets or as flashings.

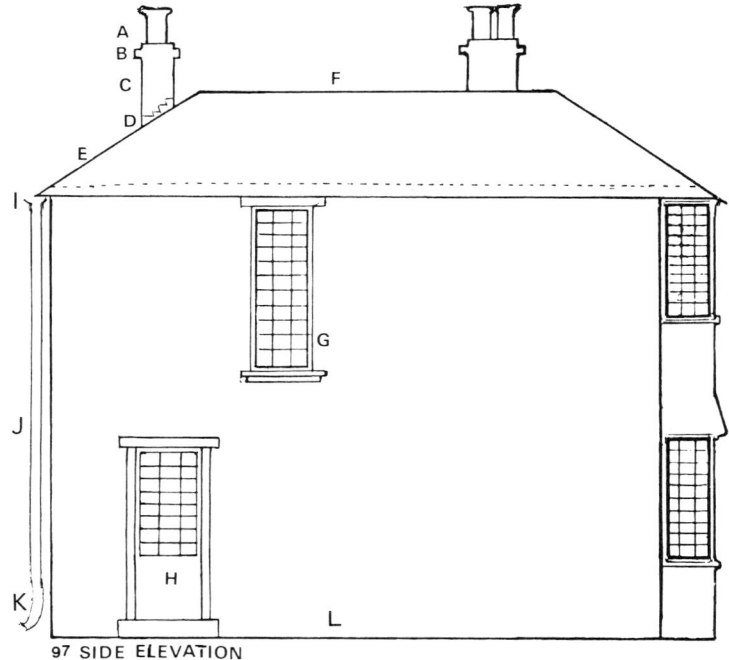

97 SIDE ELEVATION

97 A Is the chimney pot broken?
B Is the flaunching in good order?
C Is the pointing sound?
D Is the flashing sound?
E Are the ridge tiles all right?
F How about the other tiles in the roof?
G Do the windows leak?
H How does the door let in water?
I How is the guttering? Does it need renewing?
J And how about the downpipe?
K And the spout?

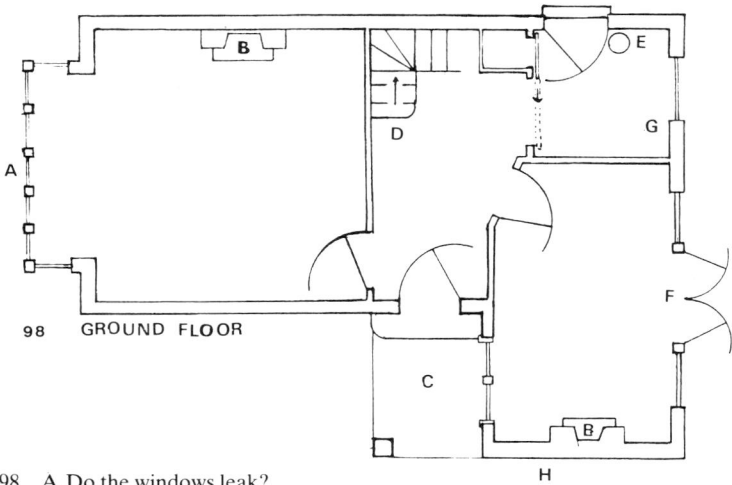

98 GROUND FLOOR

98 A Do the windows leak?
    B Are the fireplaces in good order? And the chimney?
    C Does the porch let in water?
    D Are the stairs sound? Or do they creak?
    E Does the kitchen stove work properly? And the other kitchen apparatus?
    F Are the doors to the garden sound?
    G Is the wash basin sound? And the pipework?
    H Is the damp proof course sound?

Formwork

Scaffolding formwork access and ancillary equipment all play their part in the renovation of old buildings. Decking systems are also obviously important, be they purchased or hired. There are plywood systems which may serve the purpose. But do not stint on formwork and remember that accidents in the building trade are very common.

Water features

Fountains, waterfalls and the like are perhaps more in the sphere of the landscape gardener than the builder. Nevertheless there may be occasions when such comes the builders way. There are fountain kits to be made up or some customers want special ideas carried out.

Garages

While many people want a garage built in the same style as their homes and with similar materials there is also a thriving market for kit built garages. In some cases the firm supplying the parts will also erect the garage but otherwise a local builder will undertake this. Full working instructions and diagrams are supplied with the parts. These remarks also apply to garden sheds, summer houses and the like. Where planning permission is needed the company supplying the garage usually deals with the authorities.

Grilles

Grilles and security grilles are produced by several manufacturers whose literature illustrates the various items in their ranges. Such makers also usually produce a variety of other products such as, for example, doors and shutters, roller shutters, sectional doors and overhead doors, fire resisting doors, collapsible gates, traffic booms, electrically operated gates and movable partitions.

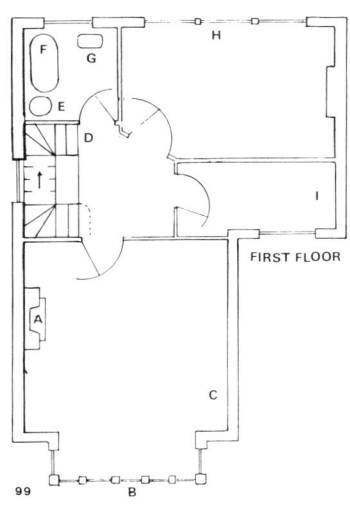

FIRST FLOOR

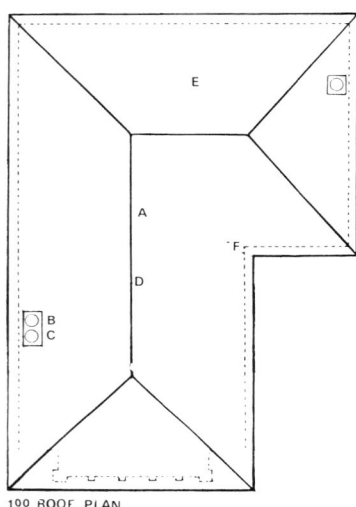

100 ROOF PLAN

99 First floor
   A Fireplace — is it in good order and what about the chimney?
   B Do the windows leak?
   C Is the wall damp?
   D Is the landing satisfactory? Is it damp?
   E How is the WC?
   F And the bath?
   G What about the basin?
   H Is the window ill fitting or does it fit properly?
   I Does the radiator keep the place warm when warmth is required?
100   Roof plan
   A Are the ridge tiles sound?
   B Is the chimney pot all right?
   C What about the chimney itself?
   D In what condition are the roof tiles?

Handrails and balstrades

Several firms produce handrails, balustrades, spiral staircases and balconies. These can be made in wood, metal or both. In the case of the spiral staircases very accurate measurements are needed and most companies send their own representatives to the site to measure up.

Kitchen furniture

There has been a revolution in kitchens during the last few years and a great many very attractive designs have come from overseas, particularly from Germany.

The components of the modern kitchen are usually produced on a factory basis and they are chosen to fit whatever space is required to be filled. Such schemes produce excellent results and prove very popular with young married couples. Draining board units, cupboards, alcoves, projections, penisula runs and corner arrangements are all well catered for by such systems. So are cooker canopies. Special kitchen tiles are produced and there is cooperation between manufacturers of cooking appliances over the dimensions to which kitchen units should be made.

Ladder, trestles and platforms

In addition to the conventional ladder of wood the light weight aluminium ladders are increasingly popular because they represent a saving in weight and are easier to erect. Other ladders include extending loft ladders, free standing ladders, double sided ladders and glass fibre construction ladders for use in hazardous areas. Closely allied to ladders are spring loaded trap doors and platforms for working on.

Porches

Porches are available in flat pack form which come with easy instructions for assembly. Both glass porches are available and also solid timber ones. Plastic is also used. Some of these porches have brickwork at the lower part and there is usually a choice of doors and door furniture.

Roof lights

Roof lights may be of wood or metal, both aluminium or steel. For curved roof lights in high yield steels there are lengths curved about major or minor axes. It is also possible to have small angles up to the deepest universal beams.

Sanding equipment

Belt profile sanding machines and edgebanders are available together with straight edges using a variety of width belts on plywood, veneers or solid timber. Modern belts and various styled backing pads support long oscillating rotating belts which can produce satisfactory sanding for the most complicated profiles: There are also wide belt sanders and circular workpiece sanders, together with edgebanders.

Saunas

In the luxury bathroom trade there is a growing demand for saunas and mini sauners and the colour range is now extended and two tone products

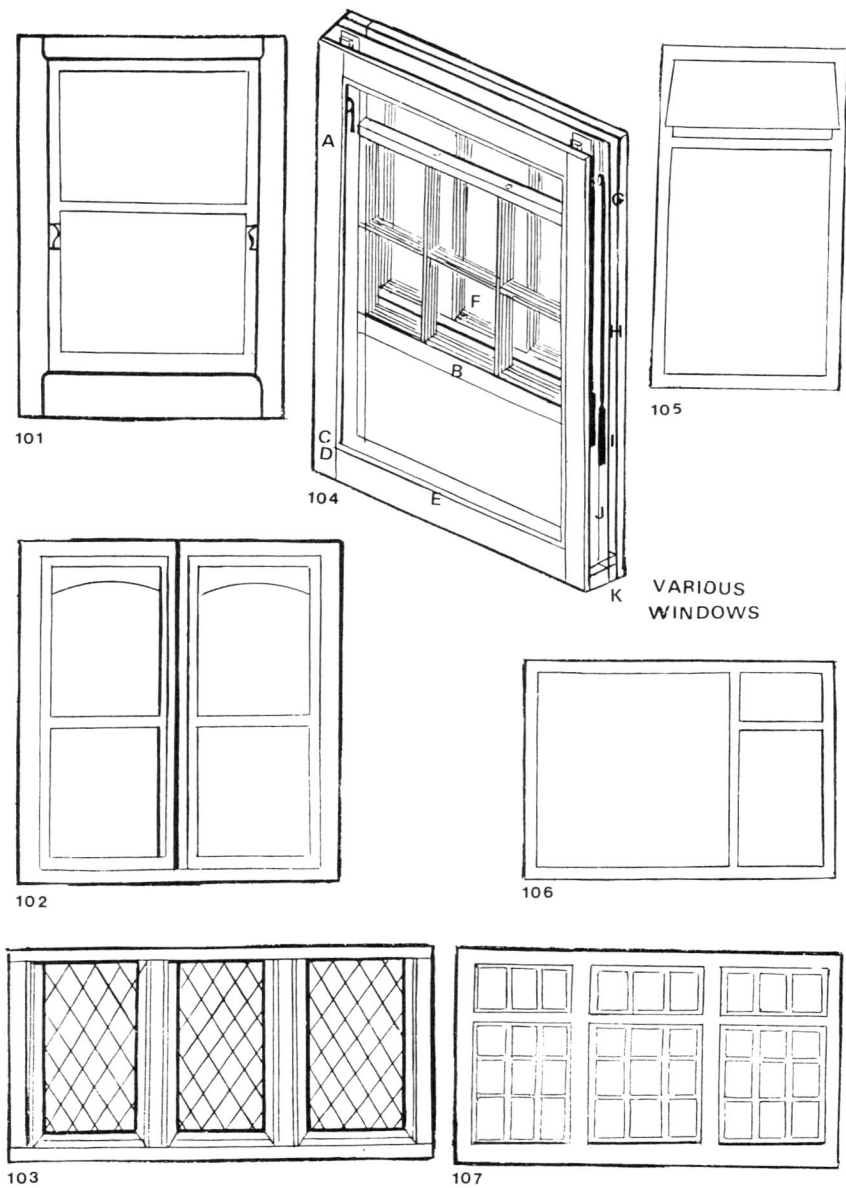

101

102

103

104

A
B
C
D
E
F
G
H
J
K

VARIOUS
WINDOWS

105

106

107

Various windows.
Sash window (101) with the horns pointing downwards.
Casement windows with arch top members (102).
Leaded lights (103).
Box framed windows (104) Double hung.
  A Inner lining
  B Meeting rail.
  C Access to weights.
  D Staff bead.
  E Draught preventers.
  F 12 lights.
  G Lining.
  H Parting member.
  I Sash balancing weight.
  J Stile for pulley.
  K Sill.
Window with upper opening (105).
Modern window (106).
Casement window with 36 lights (107).

are now available. There are also whirlpools and circular baths not to mention corner baths. Bidets are also readily available from a number of manufacturers.

Sewage treatment

Pipes for drainage may be of plastic or clay. New on the market is a 225mm diameter plain end sleeve jointed pipe which is said to be the logical way of connecting round the house drainage to the main sewer. The sewer coupling is believed to eliminate mess with broken pipes and live pipe connections when doing up old property it is often necessary to mend sewers and there are now means of achieving this without too much trouble.

Staircases

Standard and made-to-measure staircases are available in different woods such as oak, yellow or red exotic wood or beech. Standard staircases are produced on a modular system. Banisters which are either chamfered or turned are obtainable and stair treads may be had either with or without risers.

Windows

Windows come in many standard sizes and are available in timber or plastic as well as metal. Individual windows can be produced if required but obviously, these are going to cost more than standard windows. Double glazing has produced a revolution in good window design and these units too are obtainable in standard sizes. There are mock leaded lights which look very like the real thing.

Chapter 6
TOOLS AND EQUIPMENT

Many of the tools and items of equipment used by the building trades concerned with new construction are also suitable for the repair and maintenance of houses. However there are some older tools which may be unknown to the younger generation so these may be mentioned here. Also even today's tools and equipment deserve some recognition and these are also mentioned. As far as possible the items discussed here are grouped into their own trades but, on occasion, this is rather less than satisfactory and so, in some instance there may be cases where a particular item appears to have strayed out of context. When this happens the reason is usually because the item could well appear under more than one heading.

The bricklayers tools

The bricklayer uses a number of tools the principal ones being as follows:

The trowels which lay and spread the mortar on which the bricks are laid and which point up the joints later. Trowels are handed, i.e., they are made for right-handed or left-handed bricklayers. Usually they are ten to thirteen inches in length. Pointing trowels are much smaller; they vary from two inches to about eight inches and they are used for pointing and for small work. Pointing trowels are used with hawks which are square pieces of wood or metal with a gripping handle beneath. The hawk is designed to hold the mortar when the bricklayer is doing pointing.

The plum rule is a piece of equipment which has nearly become obsolete. When it was in use it consisted of a length of pine wood about five or six feet in length, about four inches wide and nearly an inch thick. The two sides were parallel and down the centre there was a line marked on the face running from the top to almost the bottom. At about nine inches from the bottom there was a bob hole the outline of which was approximately five eighths of an inch wide and some inch and a half longer than the bob.

Plumb bobs were of various sizes and were usually made of lead. For internal work they might be some three pounds in weight but for the exterior work they could be up to ten pounds. The bob string was of whip cord and it passed through a hole of some one eighth of an inch diameter and was held fast in two slots at the top. Today this tool has been superseded by the plumb level or vertical level. This usually measures some forty-eight inches long although smaller ones may be used. It is

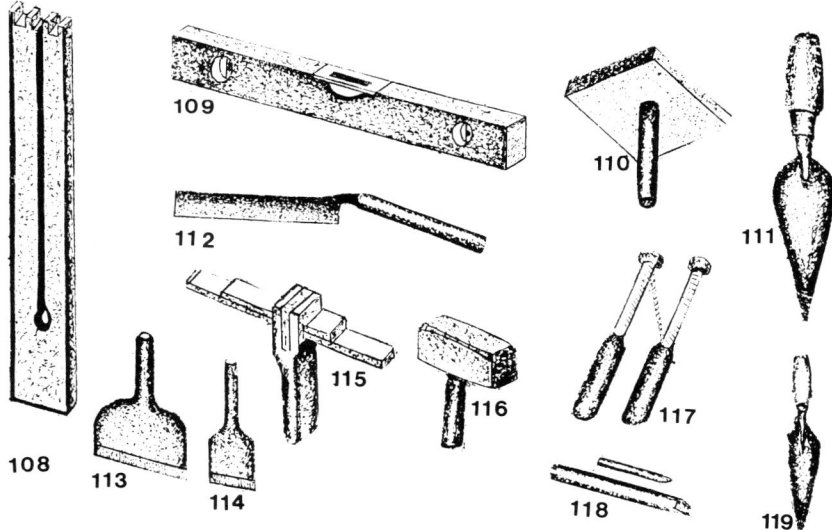

Bricklayers use a number of tools which are traditional. These include the following:
Plumb rule (108) made traditionally of pine and about two metres long with a weight varying from between three and ten pounds. The bob string should be whipcord.
Spirit level both vertical and horizontal. (109).
Hawk (110) for carrying mortar.
Brick trowel (111) for applying mortar.
Jointer (112) Used for pointing and jointing.
Boaster (113) Used for cutting bricks.
Boaster (114) for cutting chases.
Bricklayers soutch (115) A double edged chisel in a stock.
Club hammer (116) of about 4 lbs, used with a chopping block (not shown).
Line and pins (117) for setting out courses of bricks straight.
Chisel and point (119) used mainly for cutting chases.

usually made of hardwood or plastic; some are of metal and have two plumbs; there is also likely to be a single level and a couple of hand holes.

The bricklayer also uses lines and pins. The pins are inserted into the mortar to ensure that the bricks are laid properly. If the length is very long indeed a small piece of copper or zinc called a tingle is used to hold it up properly when it is stretched. This has two grooves in one end and takes the sag out of the line.

For setting out his work on old property the bricklayer should still use a two foot rule, a measuring rod and a gauge or storey rod. In southern England the gauge is four courses of brickwork to the foot, but in the north four courses rise thirteen inches.

In some cases the bricks have to be cut to shape. This is called axed work. For this the tools traditionally used are the tin saw with which the outline to be cut is marked, the required shape being cut in to the brick about a quarter of an inch. Then the unwanted parts of the brick are knocked off with a boaster which is a short, broad chisel with an inch cutting edge. This edge is slightly rounded and a club hammer is used for hitting the chisel. This hammer should weigh 4lbs. The brick is held in a chopping block which is made of two blocks of wood fastened to a base to form an angle at which it is to be held. The mass of the brick is cut off with a bricklayers axe or scutch. A scutch is a double edged chisel approximately an inch wide which fits into a stock and is held in position by a wedge.

For the softer kinds of brick which are sometimes used for gauged work an old tenon saw may be used. Alternatively it is sometimes possible to fix up something which consists of an old bow frame used with a blade consisting of a couple of wires twisted together and strained so that they are of the right tension. Such a tool may be used for cutting bricks to the required shape. They are then finished by rubbing on a slab of York stone.

For cutting chases in walls the cold chisel is used while the plugging chisel comes in handy for cutting out holes in brickwork and for such purposes as cutting out joints for lead flashings. Also used for jointing brickwork is the jointer. This has a blade of steel between two and six inches long which may be grooved, flat, concave or convex. Another tool which was used for jointing was the pointing rule. This consisted of a length of wood some three inches by seven eighths which was bevelled on one edge.

To this were fixed distance pieces. Many of the older bricklayers made themselves frenchmen which was a tool cut to shape from an old table knife. This was cut to a point on both sides and then filed to a bevel edge. At the point it was bent at right angles to the blades. This home made tool was used when the bricklayer was tuck pointing. Sometimes the square was used; this was made of steel and the blade was about six inches long and the stock some four inches.

The traditional material for the bricklayer's straight edge was yellow pine and it was generally some three inches by three quarters of an inch and about three feet six inches long. Both edges were shot as they had to be parallel. Today, of course, plastic has become the material for a great many tools and it serves its purpose very well.

Masons tools

For stone which is too heavy to be lifted by hand a crane is used for placing it. A sling chain is passed around rough blocks. This has a ring at one end and a hook at the other. The hook is passed through the ring and attached to the crane or whatever kind of lifting gear is used. For stones which are already dressed sling chains are not really suitable as they may spoil the arrises unless these are protected by strips of wood or similar substances.

Dogs (or chain dogs) are short irons which are more likely to be used for lifting worked stone. These have a bridle chain passing through rings. When the crane pulls the chain exerts a tightening action and draws the dogs together. In each end of the stone a small hole is made to take the point of the dog. This is called a dog hole. Such holes are positioned as far from the top as the dog will permit.

Usually the lewis is an iron wedge. It is formed in three pieces and these fit into a hole in the top of the stone. In some lewises the two outside pieces are wedge shaped while the centre piece has its sides parallel. When in use the two wedge shaped side pieces are inserted first and the centre piece follows. At the top there is a hole through which a shackle and pin are passed. Alternatively the centre piece is wedge shaped and the side pieces are parallel. At the top they are connected with traverse pieces and they are hinged to these. At the bottom of the hole the lewis must fit tight but there can be a little free play at the top. For stones which do not weigh too much a chain lewis may be used. They fit easily and they consist of a pair of legs and a ring at the top. As the chain draws tight the legs press against the sides of the hole. This hole may be slightly undercut to provide a firm grip.

When lifting pins are used holes are cut into the top of the block at an angle of 45 degrees sloping towards the centre of the stone. The lifting pins consist of a pair of two cylindrical legs and these are inserted into the holes. As the chain draws tight these legs pull together enabling them to grip the sides of the holes. For cutting lewis holes a lewis tool is used.

For setting out the work the mason undertakes tools consisting of a 2 foot rule and a wooden straight edge which has a splayed edge are required. The compass may be from six inches to twenty four inches long; it should have a graduated wing and clamp screw to enable the legs to be set to whatever opening is required. For setting out larger circles trammel heads or beam compasses are needed.

The stock of a masons square is generally about two thirds the length of the blade. The square is made of thin steel plate. Such squares may be of various sizes but a size commonly found is twenty four inches by eighteen inches. The blade must be at right angles to the stock, if it is not, there will be problems. In sinkings where it is not possible to use an ordinary masons square a sinking square must be used. This may also measure depth. The stock, which is made of brass, is slotted to take the blade which may be clamped at whatever position is required.

Snips are used for cutting zinc moulds while bradawls, files and scribes may be needed for smoothing the moulds at their edges or in the case of bradawls, for pricking the shape of a drawing through the zinc. Bevels

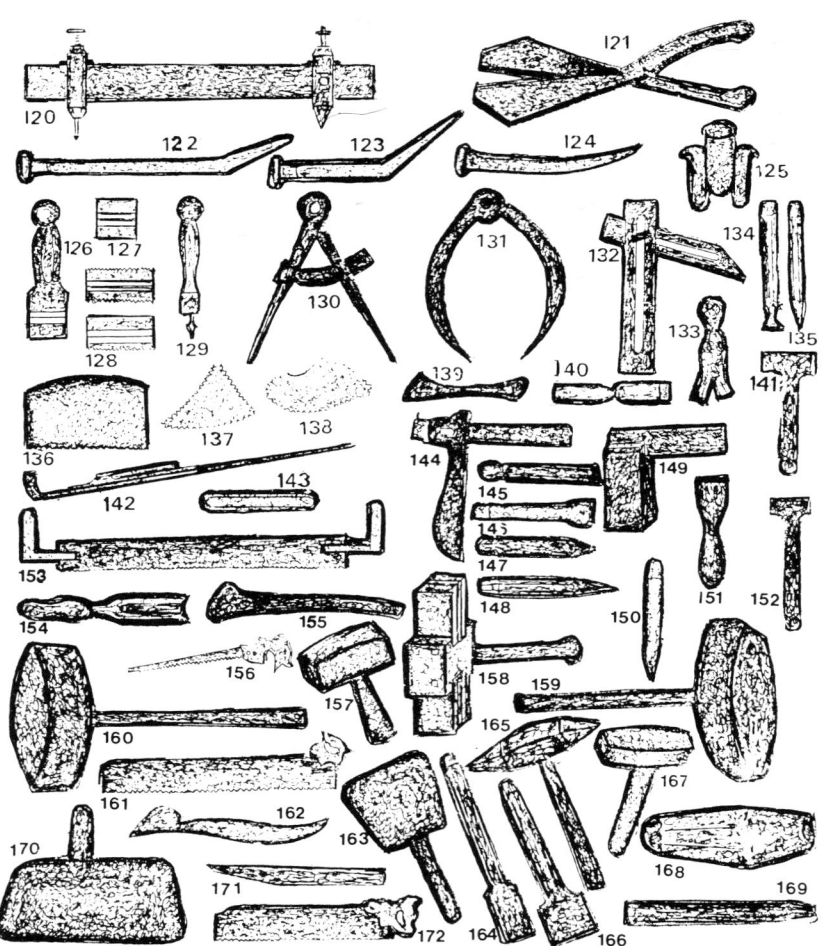

MASONS TOOLS

The masons craft is very traditional and in spite of the introduction of machinery, many of the old tools are still used. These include the following.

Trammel head and rod This is sometimes known as a beam compass (120).
Snips (121) Used for cutting zinc mould cutting.
Bent tools (122, 123 and 124) for shaping.
Plug and feathers (125) Used for splitting stone.
Faulds holder (126) Used for cutting.
Chisel (127) Used for cutting.
Double sided claw (128).
Side elevation of 126 (129).
Compasses (130)
Callipers (131) for accurate measurements around stone.
Bevel (132) The bevel is to measure angles etc. Sometimes called shift stock.
Waster (133) Little used today but not quite obsolete.
Lewising tools (134 and 135).
Drag (136) for scraping.
Cocks combs (137 and 138) for scraping and finishing.
Riffler (139).
Chisel (140).
Broad tool (141) Used like a boaster.
Trammel and scriber (142) for setting out.
Round nose (143).
Sinking square (144) Used in sinkings where ordinary squares cannot be used.
Point (145).
Chisel (146).
Point (147).
Punch (148).
Square (149) For measuring right angles.
Punch (150).
Chisel (151).
Boaster (152).
Cross cut saw (153) for soft stone.
Gouge (154).
Riffler (155).
Saw (156).
Iron hammer (157) Used for marble and by stone carvers.
Patent axe (158) Has a double edged head and is used to chop around the drafts.
Axe (159) Used on granite.
Spalling hammer (160) a double handed tool used for spalling off waste stone.
Saw (161) for soft stone.
Riffler (162).
Dummy (163) Made of zinc or lead and is about 3lbs. Used for striking tools with wooden handles.
Chisel (164).
Pick (165) Used for taking off stone which is unwanted.
Boaster (166).
Iron hammer (167).
Wedge (168) Sometimes called a gad.
Splitter (169).
Mallet (170).
Pitching tool (171).
Saw (172) for soft stone.

(sometimes called "shift stocks") are usually made of brass although they may also be made of steel. The slotted blade slides between the blades of the stock which are double. To enable the blade to be fitted at whatever angle is required there is a clamp screw.

A box trammel usually has a wooden stock with a square steel rod with its end turned down. This blade is generally a quarter inch steel. The tool is used for drawing lines parallel to the circular face. The mason also uses various straight edges with splayed edges, gauges, templates and moulds. There are also reverses for testing circular mouldings.

A number of wedges are used by the mason. These are used for coping or splitting the freestone. The top and two sides of such stone are grooved and the wedges are inserted in the grooves thus made. The stone is then placed on an iron bar and the wedges driven in until the stone splits.

For splitting granite what is known as the "plug and feathers" is used. These are inserted into the drill holes which are usually three quarters of an inch in diameter. These holes are generally about three inches and they are about four inches apart. The plug goes in first and then the feathers and the plug is driven in until the stone splits.

The cutting tools a mason uses vary according to the hardness of the stone he is working. For very hard freestone or granite there is the spalling hammer, the scabbling hammer, at least three types of saw, a pitching tool and punch. Marble masons and stone carvers use the iron hammer with which they strike cup-headed tools. The spalling hammer is a two handed tool used for spalling off waste stone. Its use is generally followed by that of a pitching tool. The spalling hammer's head is concave to ensure that it has a good cutting edge and it may weigh between sixteen and thirty pounds. For removing only a little waste there is the pitching tool and the hand hammer. The scabbing hammer is smaller than the spalling hammer for it usually weighs between fourteen and twenty pounds. It has one spalling face and one pick face. A scabbing pick has two pick faces. For marble the pitching tool used may be no more than half an inch wide but it may be a couple of inches wide for softer freestones. The steel hand hammer is some seven inches long and weighs five to six pounds and it is used with the pitching tool and punch. The axe with its double edged head can be used to obtain a fairly smooth face when it cuts around the drafts. The patent axe produces an axed face on granite after the axe has been used on it. A four bladed axe is used for rough patent axe work. The pitching tool has a slightly bevelled edge about a quarter of an inch thick for marble.

Masons mallets are generally of beech or hickory. They are oval and are used for striking certain tools when freestones are worked. Dummies are usually of lead and weigh some three pounds. They are for striking wooden handled tools used in working the softer freestones. Chisels are hammer-headed, mallet headed or cup headed. Hammer headed tools have a flat head. Mallet headed tools have slender necks and rounded heads. Such tools are used for frafts and fillets while the point is for getting rid of unwanted material. Usually a tooth chisel follows in the wake of the point to reduce the surface still further. Finally the surface is finished with the boaster.

For softer freestones such as Bath or Beer wooden handled tools are often used such as drafting chisels, drivers, gauges and drags. The latter are used for finishing soft freestones. Cockscombs are rather like drags and are used to finish mitres and mouldings. For softer stones the saws mentioned earlier are used.

Carpentry and joinery

Much of the wood now employed in houses is machined and this does away with the need for many craftsmen to carry the kind of kit of tools which their grandfathers used. However when repairing old property there are occasions when it is desirable to have the tools of yesteryear for certain repair and maintenance jobs. These are discussed here. The joiner and carpenter uses many different tools and the comments made here are not intended to be exhaustive but it is hoped that they may be reasonably

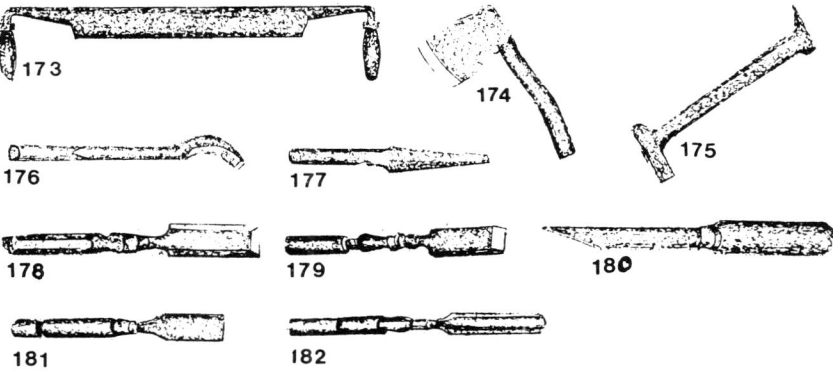

CARPENTERS TOOLS

By tradition carpenters use a great many tools for cutting, boring and impelling, a variety of wooden planes, marking out and sawing.

Draw knife (173) is sometimes used on members which are round in section and which require shaving.

Axe (174) is used for chopping trees and for bringing timber into roughly the right shape.

Drawer lock chisel forms the mortise in the door rail which receives the bolt of the drawer lock (175).

Mortice lock chisel (176) is used for mortising.

Socket chisel (177) is used for heavy work and with a socket into which the handle fits.

Pocket chisel (178) is sometimes known as a sash chisel. Their use includes cutting pockets in pulley stiles of sash frames.

Firmer chisel (179) is normally used by the joiner and can stand blows from a mallet.

Mortice chisel (180) is used for mortising.

Smaller chisel (181) also used for mortising.

Gouge (182) This type of chisel has a curved cutting edge.

comprehensive. First consider the tools used for marking and setting out.

These include rules, a marking gauge, a straight edge, try square, bevel, compass, mitre square, gauges and callipers. For rules the traditional material is boxwood and the traditional length is two feet with a four-fold construction. On such a measure, in spite of metrification, the inches are still shown and divided into sixteenths. Straight edges can be up to eight feet long and some four inches by half an inch. The try square comes in different sizes and is used for setting out right angles and making sure different surfaces are at right angles. A sliding bevel is equipped with a slotted blade which is loose; it can be set at any required angle with a thumb screw.

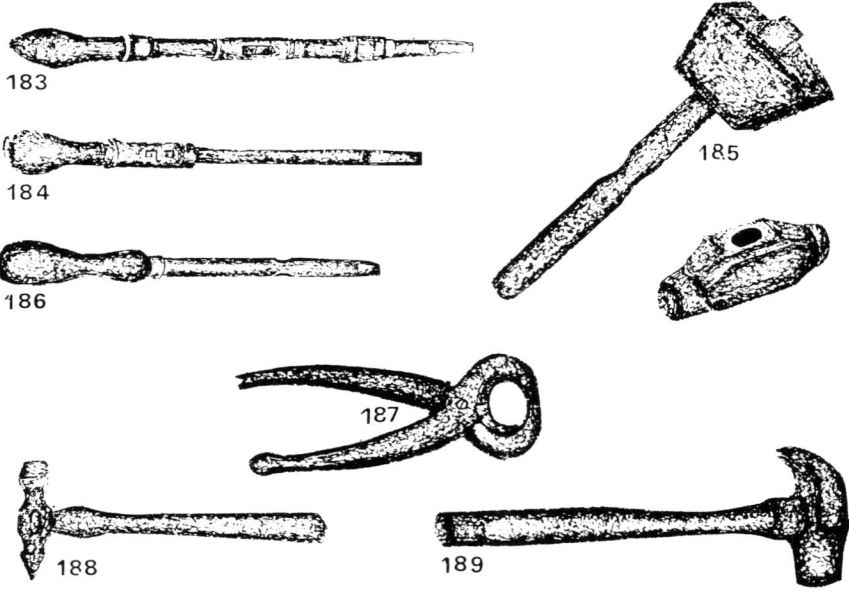

CARPENTERS TOOLS

Spiral screwdriver (183) Quickacting screwdriver.
Ratchet screwdriver (184) Easy-to-use ratchet screwdriver.
Mallet (185) Used for hitting tools and woodwork.
Screwdriver (186) Used for driving screws home and for unscrewing.
Pincers (187) For removing nails etc.
Warrington hammer (188) The head is made of cast steel to resist impact.
Claw hammer (189).

The various kinds of gauges available include the marking gauge with its marking point for drawing lines parallel with the edge of a piece of wood. The cutting gauge is rather similar except that it has a cutter in it instead of a marker; it is for cutting strips of thin wood. A mortise gauge is used where parallel lines have to be marked out as is the case with a mortise and tenon; it has a couple of marking points and these are adjustable.

The spirit level and the plumb rule are used for making sure that vertical and horizontal surfaces are true.

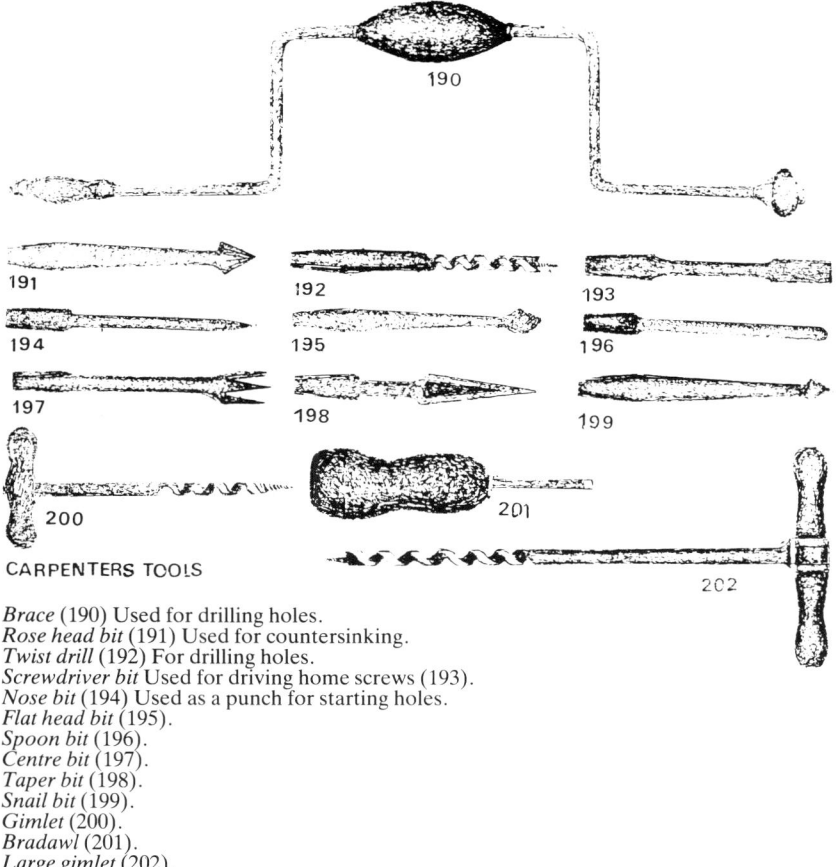

CARPENTERS TOOLS

Brace (190) Used for drilling holes.
Rose head bit (191) Used for countersinking.
Twist drill (192) For drilling holes.
Screwdriver bit Used for driving home screws (193).
Nose bit (194) Used as a punch for starting holes.
Flat head bit (195).
Spoon bit (196).
Centre bit (197).
Taper bit (198).
Snail bit (199).
Gimlet (200).
Bradawl (201).
Large gimlet (202).

Tools for planing and cutting consist of saws, planes, gauges, chisels and the spokeshave. There is a variety of saws but each is made of the best steel and is fitted with a handle which is either wood or plastic. These include the cross cut saw, the rip saw, the panel saw, the compass saw, the tenon saw, the pad saw, the hack saw, and the dovetail saw.

Cross cut saws are designed to work across the grain while the rip saw cuts along the grain. The panel saw is for very fine work such as dovetailing. In the rip saw the teeth should be about three eighths of an inch apart while those in a cross cut saw should be some quarter of an inch apart. Panel saw teeth are similar to those of the cross cut but they are very much smaller. The tenon saw is used for cutting tenons shoulders. It has a blade of between twelve and sixteen inches long and very fine teeth, usually with ten points to the inch.

The blade, which is thinner than an ordinary saw is stiffened on its upper edge by a brass or iron spline. The dovetail saw is finer than the tenon saw and is used for very fine work. For cutting curves there is the bow saw; its narrow blade is held in tension by a wooden frame and string. The alternative is to use a compass or keyhole saw which, in addition to cutting keyholes, may also be used for cutting curves. The pad saw is rather similar. Both the keyhole saw and the pad saw have one handle and a blade which tapers almost to a point. The hack saw is for cutting metal. For cutting timber there is the two handed saw with its blade between five and eight inches wide while its length may be between four and seven feet long.

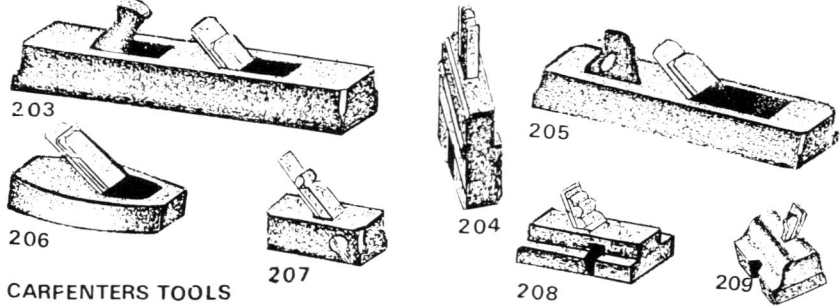

CARPENTERS TOOLS

Many of the wooden planes have gone out of fashion. They are cast aside in favour of modern instruments. But here are some the old craftsmen used.
Jack plane (203) Used for roughing off.
Grooving plane (204).
Trying plane (205).
Smoothing plane (206).
Rebate plane (207).
Hollow plane (208).
Router plane (209).

The set of a saw means the extent to which its teeth are bent to right and left alternately. This allows the blade to pass through the cut being made in the wood. Technically the 'set' refers to the extent to which the teeth bend outwards. Without this tolerance the saw would not pass freely back and forth; instead it would stick. When a saw is sharpened it is very important that the set should be retained properly.

There are four kinds of chisels; paring, firmer, mortising and gouges. Chisels come in various sizes from one sixteenth to two inches. The firmer chisel is the one usually used by the joiner. The blade is fixed into a wooden or plastic handle by a tang and it is usually formed with a shoulder to allow it to be hit by a mallet. Bevelled edged chisels usually have a thinner blade and are reserved for fine work. For mortising the thicker mortise chisel is used. Being thicker and stronger than the firmer chisel they can withstand the leverage needed for loosening the wood core when cutting a mortise. For really heavy work there used to be socket chisels which had a socket which fitted the handle. For cutting pockets in the faces of pulley stiles in sash frames there is the pocket or sash chisel.

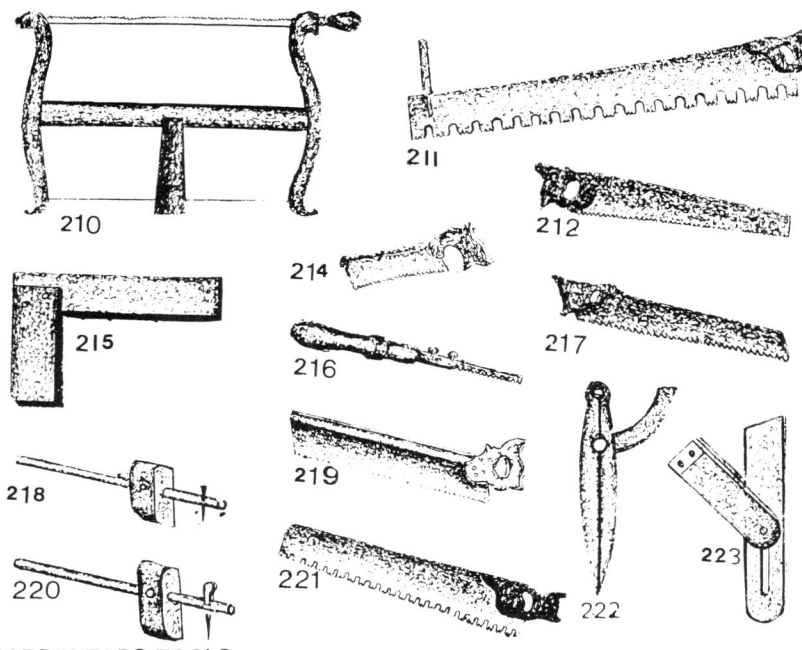

CARPENTERS TOOLS

Bow saw (210) sometimes called turning saw.
22-Man cross cut saw (211).
Cross cut saw (211).
Dove tail saw (214).
Try square (215).
Keyhole saw (216).
Rip saw (217).
Marking gauge (218).
Tenon saw (219).
Cutting gauge (220).
Farmers saw (221) for green timber or for lumber.
Compass (222).
Sliding bevel (223).

To form the mortise in the door rail which takes the bolt of the drawlock there is the draw lock chisel. If there is any waste wood to be taken away the draw knife is use. Gouges may be described as chisels with curved cutting edges. This cutting edge may be ground on either side so that they may be concave or convex.

There is a wide variety of planes, some of which are seldom used today. These include such planes as the jack plane, the trying plane and the smoothing plane. In the old days planes were usually made of wood with steel blades but today most are made of metal which wears longer, especially when used on hard wood. The old wooden plane usually had a stock of beech in which the cutting iron was fixed by means of a wedge. On the cutting iron there was a back iron which was fixed by a brass nut and screw. This back iron was meant to break the shaving as it cut and bent it over, thereby preventing the plane being choked with shavings. No doubt the back iron also helped to stiffen the cutting iron. The cutting edge of the jack plane was generally very slightly convex while that of the smoothing plane was usually straight but with the corners just very slightly rounded.

The spokeshave was used for circular work which needed fining down. For forming rebates the rebate plane was used while the plough was used for forming grooves running with the grain. To enable the depth of the rebate to be adjusted a fillister was used. The fillister had an adjustable fence which controlled its depth while the cutters at each side marked the rebate ahead of the cutting blade.

There are also metal planes which are variations on the wooden planes described. These wear better and are perhaps more accurate and they last longer, especially if worked on hardwood. In metal planes the cutter is kept in the correct position by either a screw or a lever. The latter probably gives easier and finer adjustment. Metal planes include smoothing planes, block planes which are used for very small work and bullnose planes. Bullnose planes enable wood to be planed right up to the edge.

Of the boring tools perhaps the bradawl and the gimlet are the most common. Bradawls have tiny wedge shaped cutters; they are mainly used for boring holes. Gimlets are used for boring small holes which are usually for screws. The brace and bit is really a handle; to it is attached a cutter for boring the holes. There are several different kinds of brace while bits come in different diameters. The rachet brace is the best type to use. In addition to the ordinary bit there is the spoon bit which has a projecting nose to clear the wood, and the nose bit as well as the centre bits which can be up to one and a half inches in diameter. For larger holes there are expanding bits while for tapering holes there are tapper bits.

In addition to these boring tools there are tools designed for counter sinking. These include the rose head, the flat head, and the snail head. Then there are screwdriver bits, twist drills and auger bits. In addition there are many types of electric drills which will be discussed later. One further tool deserves mention here. This is the forstner which has a circular rim instead of a point. It was used for flat bottom boring. Today this tool is little used but the reader may be able to find a forstner in a jumble sale.

The impelling tools the carpenter uses include screwdrivers, mallets and hammers. Screwdrivers are either fixed or rachet. The latter save a lot of time when repetitive work has to be undertaken. Mallets are used for driving chisels as their heads are less likely to spoil the chisel handles than hammers. Hammers come in different sizes and are used for different purposes. The club hammer is intended for heavy work. The Warrington hammer is made of cast steel and weighs about a pound.

The slater's tools

Comparatively few tools are used by the slater but those which are used are for trimming and fixing slates and for repairing roofs generally.

The zax is the tool for trimming. This is a blade fixed in a handle of wood. The zax is really a chopper with a spike on top. There is also the cutting and dressing iron which is a straight edge of iron with a couple of spikes going into a handle. The slate being dressed rests on this cutting iron which it overhangs by whatever is to be cut off. Sharp taps get rid of the unwanted slate. To measure slates a guage stick or scantle is used. The spike

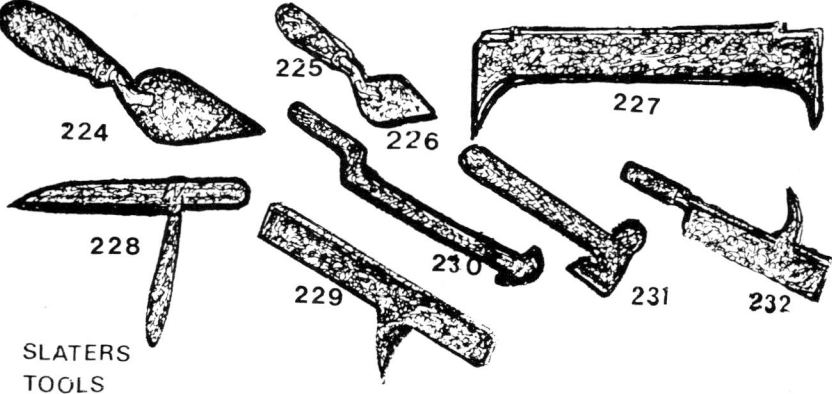

SLATERS
TOOLS

Slaters tools are used comparatively little today when the fashion is to use tiles. But anyone repairing a slate roof may be pleased to have some knowledge of these old tools.
Laying trowel (224).
Pointing trowel (225 and 226).
Cutting iron (227) Sometimes called a dressing iron.
Pick hammer (228).
Slater's iron (229).
Ripper (230).
Lath hammer (231).
Chopper (232) Sometimes called a zax.

mentioned above in connection with the zax is used to mark the position of the trimmer slate for the nail holes which are often made by a couple of sharp blows. However sometimes a holing machine is taken to the site. The hammer is broad headed for driving the nails in. It has a long metal arm and a spike at the other end for making the holes larger if necessary. The ripper is used for repairing roofs. It consists of a metal member in a wooden handle. At the other end is a cross piece forming a hook on either side of the arm. There is a cutting edge at the back. Slates are removed by passing the ripper between the slates and around the fixing nail. When the ripper is withdrawn quickly it cuts off the nail at its head thereby making it possible to remove the slate. The slater also uses a chalk line, rods and two kinds of trowels; knee pads are also used and a belt with a pocket for the nails.

The plasterer's tools
The plasterer uses several different rules and trowels. Various floats are also employed in what is certainly one of the most highly skilled crafts in the building trade.

Traditionally, pine free of knots, was used for many of the plasterers tools. The Derby is rather a long float (about four feet to perhaps eight feet) and some three to four inches wide with a couple of handles placed so that one person can hold both of them quite easily. However this tool is sometimes worked by two people. It is used for scouring and levelling ceilings and the surfaces of walls in both the floating and setting coats which are intended as a preparation for the finishing.

The floating rule may be some eight feet (up to some twenty feet) long and perhaps four to six inches wide. At the back it is tapered towards each end. It can be used for forming screeds and for the surfaces between the screeds. A traversing rule is rather like a floating rule except that it is not usually longer than six feet and it is used for forming screeds in setting plaster. The parallel rule sets out parallel lines and a levelling rule has a wooden member fixed above the lower edge of a parallel rule. A level may be set on this when a soffit has to be levelled. The plumb rule makes sure that so called 'verticals' are really vertical.

Joint rules consist of a steel strip about three inches wide and an eighth of an inch thick in a stock of hardwood. One end and the edge are splayed and the other end is finished at an acute angle. These rules are employed when mitres have to be formed in situ.

The lath or plasterer's hammer usually has a steel head and a wooden handle. At the other end there is an adze which can be used for cutting and fixing laths. There is also a slot for withdrawing nails on the lower edge.

Hand floats are available in several shapes and sizes. With the exception of the panel or float they are usually of pine and very often they are about ten and a half inches long by four and a half inches thick by three quarters of an inch. The cross grain float is somewhat similar except that it is slightly longer and thicker and is cut with the grain running across the float. There is a dovetail groove at the rear which takes a hardwood key carrying the handle. This arrangement helps to keep the float from warping. The cross grain float is used for scouring the setting coat.

A skimming float is rather like a hand float except that it is longer. It is used for laying the setting coat before laying off with a steel trowel. In a skimming float the grain of wood is parallel with the handle. For use with small panels where large tools could not be used there are margin floats which are usually made of beech. They are generally about six inches by three inches and some half inch thick.

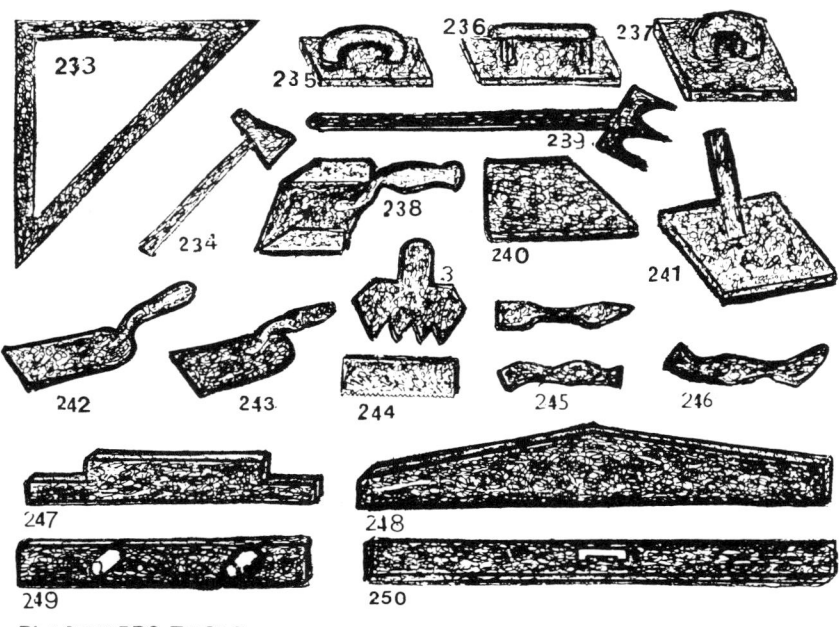

PLASTERERS TOOLS

Square (233).
Plasterers hammer (234).
Hand float (235).
Laying trowel (236).
Cross grain float (237).
Angle trowel (238) Sometimes called a twitcher.
Scratcher (239).
Joint rule (240).
Hawk (241).

Window trowel (242).
Margin trowel (243).
Drag (244).
Scratch tool (245).
Scratch tool (246).
Gauge rule (247).
Floating rule (248).
Derby float (249).
Levelling rule (250).

Hawks are usually sections of pine which are about twelve inches square and five eights of an inch thick. They have a round central hole on the underside for the handle. Scratch tools are used for working mitres, carving or refining enrichments. They very often have a shaft with a tool at each end which are serrated like saw teeth. The birch broom or scratch is used for scoring surfaces to make a key for other work. It is often made of a piece of pine about fourteen inches long by seven inches wide and half an inch thick. One of the ends is shaped while the other is cut into teeth with points about an inch and a quarter apart. Some plasterers fix two or three laths together to provide more points.

In the old days when hair was mixed with coarse stuff larries were used for the mixing. These were three pronged rakes with long wooden handles. Twiches were angle trowels some two or three inches wide with sides at right angles to the blade. This permitted the tool to be run up internal angles and to smooth both faces of the return in a single operation.

The plasterer uses several different trowels for laying and finishing the setting coats. These trowels are of different sizes and shapes. The laying trowel is rectangular and is a piece of steel between ten and eleven inches by some five inches. The handles are held firm by a couple of metal shanks. The panel trowel is very like the laying trowel except that its blade is very springy. For gauging stuff on the hawk or for laying stuff on the moulding there is the gauging trowel which is made in different sizes.

The steel square is triangular. One angle is a right angle while the other two are at forty-five degrees. The plasterer also uses planes, gauges, files, rasps, chisels, callipers, brushes, compasses, a spirit level and saws as well as other tools.

Tools for house painting

Painters tools are mainly brushes and knives. In older property there may be graining, varnishing and perhaps stippling but this is unusual today. In modern work it is usually a matter of removing existing paintwork if this is in bad condition and then repainting.

The putty or stopping knife is used to fill holes while irregularities of the surface are treated with the filling or broad knife. Sometimes these are also used for scraping. The blowlamp and stripping knife are used for removing old paints and also for removing old wallpaper after it has been wetted. A chisel knife may also be used for such purposes.

Dusting brushes are useful for removing dust on old paintwork while sand and glass paper have their place in rubbing down previous coats. These materials should also be used for rubbing down between coats, the finer grades of sandpaper being used for the later coats.

Distemper brushes may be either flat and narrow or two knot brushes between four and six inches wide. They vary in weight but it may be assumed that some 8 ounces is about average. Such brushes were once either pure bristle or a mixture of bristles and were held together by either a copper band or a copper wire. Lancashire brushes which are wider are sometimes used in the North. Some of the old Lancashire brushes were eight inches in width. Today many brushes are synthetic in that their bristles are plastic. Old distemper brushes are known as stock brushes.

The old paintbrush used to be termed a one knot brush which was ground. It was mixed bristle and was bound with copper wire. Oval brushes and round grown brushes were also made. There is also the sash tool which is string bound and was employed for cutting in paint on sashes. There are also lining and angle fitch flat brushes which are bound in ferrules of tin. Such brushes were — and still are — used for lining. There are also fitches which can be flat or round in section and these are used for decorating. Obviously the blowlamp must be included in the painter's tools.

Some modern stipplers are made of rubber but the old stippler was a brush mounted on a wooden flat with a handle shaped so that the fingers could grip it firmly. These handles were usually fixed but it was possible to buy one which could be reversed. Such brushes were made in a variety of

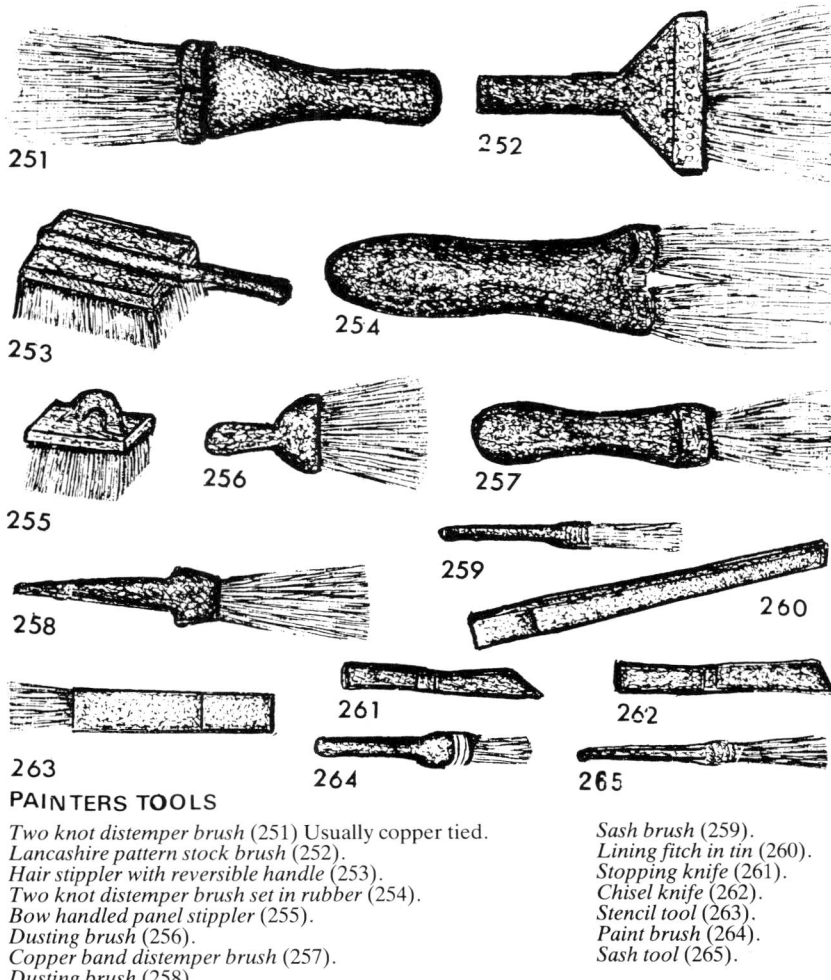

PAINTERS TOOLS

Two knot distemper brush (251) Usually copper tied.
Lancashire pattern stock brush (252).
Hair stippler with reversible handle (253).
Two knot distemper brush set in rubber (254).
Bow handled panel stippler (255).
Dusting brush (256).
Copper band distemper brush (257).
Dusting brush (258).

Sash brush (259).
Lining fitch in tin (260).
Stopping knife (261).
Chisel knife (262).
Stencil tool (263).
Paint brush (264).
Sash tool (265).

sizes. Probably comparatively few are sold today as stipple has gone out of fashion. The same applies to graining tools. At one time graining was very popular, especially in public houses, and the grainer was considered a very highly skilled member of his craft. Oval graining and graining combs were used and many craftsmen fixed up their own devices for graining. The varnishing brush is oval in section and it has white bristles.

The plumber's tools

Mallets come in different sizes and are used for bossing lead. Usually they are made of boxwood but other materials may sometimes be used. Dressers are also made of boxwood although some are made of hornbeam. Like mallets they come in different sizes. Hornbeam dressers are used for general work while boxwood dressers are mainly used for finishing. The handles should be well pitched to protect the hands of the user. The step setter or setting in stick is rather similar except that the underside is grooved to fit over the lead in setting or bending the top of the steps in step work.

Box wood is also used for making bending sticks. These are broad and rounded and are used mainly for driving lead when bends have to be made in pipes. Bossing sticks are very like bending sticks except that they are narrower and more rounded. Such bossing sticks are used for working lead round rolls. They also get well into the corners of gutters when necessary. Dummies are lead lumps at the end of a straight or curved piece of iron. They are shaped to take the dents out of pipes. Some dummies have straight handles of malacca cane.

The plumber's hammer has a head for driving nails and a nose with a thin edge for running between edges which have to be soldered. Driving wedges are quite straight but chase wedges come in various sizes and shapes. These are known as front bent or side bent depending on their shape.

Bobbins are semi oval in shape; they are made of boxwood and are put into pipes which are to be bent. To drive them round a bend a follower is used. Mandrils are smaller in diameter than pipes in which they are used. The object is to leave the interior of the pipe perfectly cylindrical so that the flow of water is not interrupted. They taper slightly to allow for withdrawal.

The plumber uses several different kinds of knives; the clasp knife; the draw knife (an instrument for two men to use for cutting up lead); a hacking knife for removing putty. There is also the bending pin which is used for making openings for branch joints. As a preparation for soldering shavenhooks are used for shaving surfaces to be soldered. Ladles carry liquid lead or solder. At one time soldering irons were much used. Today they are replaced by blowlamps which now heat solder. Electric soldering irons are popular and they are comparatively easy to work.

The plumber's saw tapers slightly; it has coarse teeth on one side and fine teeth on the other. Soldering irons are of two types; straight bits and rachet bits. Snips are used for cutting sheet metal. Step turners are used for pushing the upper edge of step flashing into brickwork. There are also rasps, the steel square, the straight edge, scribing gauges, the solder pot and the rule.

Electrical tools

So much for the tools of yesteryear, many of which are still in use today and any of which may prove useful when doing up old buildings. As the reader knows there are modern power tools which have, in part, replaced some of the older hand tools. These include electric saws, sanders, drills and a variety of useful machines. These are so well known to readers that it is unnecessary to dwell on them here in a book concerned with the repair and maintenance of old houses.

Appendix I
NAMES AND ADDRESSES OF POSSIBLE INTEREST TO READERS

A selection of companies, firms and craftsmen who, while undertaking general building work in many cases, are believed to specialise in the repair and maintenance of period houses, or in supplying materials and items required for such work. While reasonable care has been undertaken in compiling this list, because circumstances may change frequently, neither the author nor the publishers are to be held to be responsible if the information is not correct when the list is consulted.

Readers are advised to consult *Yellow Pages* for additional names in their own vicinities. In many editions of *Yellow Pages* the following categories are likely to be of interest: architectural decoration; architectural and general joinery; architectural ironmongery; architectural metal work; brick merchants; builders, bricklayers; builders' hardware; builders' merchants; building cleaning; building maintenance and repairs; concrete (ready mix); damp proofing control; dampcourse manufacture; diy wholesalers and retailers; door hardware; door manufacture (domestic); double glazing materials; drain, pipe and sewer cleaning; dry rot control; floor repair; insulation installers; interior designers; ironwork; ladder hire; maintenance services; masonry; moundings; paint removers and solvent manufacturers; pavement lights; plastering and screeding; plumbing supplies; roof lights and skylights; rot proofing; rust proofing; scaffolding hire; staircases (metal); staircases (wooden); timber merchants; window manufacturers.

LONDON

Abatiss Limited
35 Sutton Lane, London W4   01-994-2316
Treatment for dry rot, damp and woodworm. Precautions against bird damage.

Albion Design
12 Flitcroft Street, London WC2H 8DJ   01-379-7359
Cast and wrought ironwork, including Victorian type staircases.

Amazing Grates
61 High Road, London N2   01-883-9590
Specialists in restoring cast iron fireplaces; reproduction fireplaces and fenders.

Barber, Wilson and Company Limited
Crawley Road, London N22 6AH   01-888-2041
Period sanitary fittings, especially Edwardian designs.

Christopher Wray's Lighting Emporium Limited
600 Kings Road, London SW6 2DX   01-736-8434
Period internal/external electric light fittings.

J. G. McDonoigh Limited
347 New Kings Road, London SW6 4RS   01-736-7190
Fibrous plaster mouldings.

G. J. Green and Veronese
24 Edison Road, Crouch End, London N8 8AE   01-348-4462
Fibrous plaster mouldings.

Homeguard Limited
80-84 St. Mary Road, Walthamstow, London E17 9RE   01-520-4464
Repairs to doors, doorframes, windows and sashes etc.

George Jackson and Sons Limited
Rathbone Works, Rainvill Road, London W6 9MD   01-381-5297
Fibrous plaster mouldings.

Killby and Gayford Limited
44-46 Borough Road, London SE1   01-928-2732
Wood restorers and the conservation and refurbishment of period houses.

Knobs and Knockers
36 York Way, London N1   01-833-0841
Door furniture.

Langley London Limited
The Roofing Centre, 161-167 Borough High Street, London SE1   01-739-0448
Clay roofing tiles.

Locks and Handles
8 Exhibition Road, London SW7 2HF   01-584-6800
Door furniture.

London Architectural Salvage and Supply Company
St Michaels Church, Mark Street, near Paul Street, London EC2   01-247-6544
Wide variety of items from period buildings.

London Stone Limited
34 Clifton Street, London EC2A 4RU   01-247-6544
Specialists in marble and soft stone.

Metalcraft (Tottenham) Limited
6 Durnford Street, London N15 5NQ   01-802-1715
Wrought and cast iron work.

Ken Negus Limited
44 South Side, Clapham Common, London SW4 9BL   01-720-2938
Stone cleaning; also cleaning service for brick, marble, terra cotta, terrazzo and
granite.

W. H. Newson and Sons Limited
61 Pimlico Road, London SW1W 8NF   01-730-6262
Specialists in period joinery, mouldings and windows.

T. Peppiatt and Sons Limited
Elizabeth Works, 32 The Grangeway, London N21   01-360-8081
Restoration of historic buildings and special joinery.

Rominar Limited
106 Columbia Road, London E2   01-739-4168
Stone cleaning service.

W. Sitch and Company
48 Berwick Street, London W1V 3RA   01-437-3776
Restorers and makers of reproduction period electric light fittings.

Sitting Pretty
131 Dawes Road, London SW6 7EA   01-381-0049
Period taps, basins and wcs. Edwardian type shower fittings and taps.

Southwell (Stockwell) Limited
Arch 166, Steedman Street, London SE17   01-703-7740
Coast iron works.

The Stove Shop
181 Kings Cross Road, London WC1   01-833-3534
Antique and period stoves.

Thomas and Wilson Limited
454 Fulham Road, London SW6 1BY   01-381-1161
Fibrous plaster mouldings.

Wandles Workshop
200 Garret Lane, London SW18   01-870-5873
Restoration specialists in period fireplaces and mantlepieces.

J. Whitehead and Sons Limited
Imperial Works, 64 Kennington Oval, London SE11 5SP   01-735-1602
Stone restoration specialists.

Yannedis and Company Limited
25-27 Theobalds Road, London WC1X 8SR   01-242-7106
Ironmongery.

OUTSIDE LONDON

For easy reference the following places are listed below in alphabetical order.

Accrington
Accrington Brick and Tile Company Limited
Nori Works, Accrington, Lancashire BB5 5DR   0254-32684
Brick and tile manufacturers.

Angus
John Strathearn and Son Limited
40 Roods, Kirriemuir, Angus   0575-72163
Maintenance and restoration; stone masonry; carpentry, joinery, plumbing and electrical work.

Ashbourne
A. F. Yeomans and Sons
1 Birches Terrace, Ashbourne, Derbyshire DE6 1ED   0335-42709
Brickwork, masonry. Reroofing in tiles, Welsh slate or stone slates. Treatment for woodworm, dry rot and damp. Repair and replacement of structural timber. Moundings, doors and window frames.

Aylmerton
Robert Mallett
The Bays, The Street, Aylmerton, Norfolk NR11 8AA   026-375-569
General maintenance and specialist in renovating period property.

Bampton
John Fryer
Waits Farm, Ashton, Bampton, Oxford OX8 2DN   0993-850320
Specialist in work on period houses. Restoration and renovation of stone houses. Conversions undertaken.

Bangor
Penrhyn Quarries Limited
Bethesda, near Bangor, Gwynedd LL57 4YG   0248-600-656
Stone.

Barnsley
Carlton Main Brickworks
Grimethorpe, near Barnsley, South Yorkshire S72   0226-711521
Bricks.

Barnsley
Yorkshire Brick Company
Wombwell Lane, Stairfoot, Barnsley, South Yorkshire S70 3NS   0226-283114
Bricks.

Bath
Edwin J. Cooper (Builder) Limited
24 Smallcombe Close, Clandown, Redstock, Bath, Avon BA3 3BD   0761-32463
Renovating period houses.

Bath
George V. William and Sons Limited
Windsor Bridge Road, Bath, Avon BA2 3DT   0225-22286
Specialists in Combe Down stone, wrought iron work and lead. Stone cleaning
service. Drawing office facilities.

Beccles
Dopson Builders Limited
1 Grove Mews, Ingate, Beccles, Suffolk NR34 9RZ   0502-715301
Period restoration and renovation including design when required. Period joinery
and fibrous plaster work.

Bedford
London Brick Company Limited
Stewartby, Bedfordshire MK43   0234-851851
Bricks.

Bishop Auckland
William Allison and Sons Limited
7 South Church Road, Bishop Auckland, Durham   0388-603245
Specialists in restoring historic buildings. Stone cut to size. Mouldings, cutting
lettering etc.

Bristol
A. E. Rollin and Sons
49 Nicholls Lane, Winterbourne, Bristol, Avon   0454-773684

Bristol
Almondsbury Forge Works Limited
Sundays Hill, Almondsbury, Bristol BS12 4DS   0454-613315
Reproduction ornamental ironwork, railings, balustrades, firebaskets and
architectural ironwork.

Cambridge
Rattee and Kett Limited
Purbeck Road, Cambridge CB2 2PG   0223-48061
Specialists in stone masonry and joinery.

Cheltenham
Architectural Heritage of Cheltenham
Boddington Manor Stables, Boddington Lane, Cheltenham   024-268-741
Specialists in salvaged materials.

Darwen
Shaw's of Darwen (Ceramics) Limited
Waterside, Darwen, Lancashire BB3 3NX   0254-71811
Terra Cotta mouldings.

East Cowes, Isle of Wight
R. Rann
The Forge, Whippingham, East Cowes, Isle of Wight   0983-292716
Blacksmith and engineering; stairs, gates, balustrades etc.

Edinburgh
J. G. Coleman
3 Hillside Crescent, Edinburgh EH7 5DY   031-556-2664
Restoring period houses.

Edinburgh
Waterblasters
35B Ferry Road, Edinburgh EH6   031-553-4993
Stone cleaning and restoration work.

Edinburgh
W. and J. R. Watson (Stonecraft) Limited
Romano House, Station Road, Edinburgh EH12 7AQ   031-334-9871

Exeter
M. D. Shervington
95 Broadway, St Thomas, Exeter, Devon EX2 9LZ   0392-51681
Special windows and doors. Georgian style sliding sash windows and panel doors.

Exeter
Westbrick Limited
Pinhoe, Exeter EX4 8JT   0392-66561
Bricks.

Glasgow
Restore and Stone (Scotland) Limited
Garscube Mill, Killermont Bridge, Bearsden, Glasgow G4   041-942-9008
Masonry restoration; stone.

Houghton-le-Spring
Lumley Brickworks Limited
Woodstone Village, Houghton-le-Spring, Tyne and Wear   0385-852361
Bricks.

Knaresborough
Hamley Aagaard Limited
Frogmore House, Stockwell Road, Knaresborough HG5 0JP   0532-568678
Specialist in fibrous plaster work.

Leicester
Ibstock Building Products Limited
Ibstock, Leicester LE6 1HS   0530-60531
Bricks.

Manchester
Thomas Mosedale and Sons Limited
Flixton Brick Works, Carrington Road, Flixton, Lancashire   061-748-2050
Bricks.

Measham
Red Bank Manufacturing Company Limited
Measham, near Burton-on-Trent, Staffordshire DE12 7EL   0530-70333
Ceramic building components and materials; traditional ridge tiles; traditional
finials. Reputed to be the largest manufacturers of clay chimney pots in Europe.

Newbury
Water Reed Thatchers
The Gardens, Hamstead Marshall, near Newbury, Berkshire   04885-8816
Traditional Norfolk reed and wheat thatching.

Newcastle
Steetley Brick Limited
PO Box No 3, Brampton Hill, Newcastle, Staffordshire ST5 0QU   0782-615381
Bricks.

Nottingham
Nottingham Brick PLC
Dorket Head, Arnold, Nottingham NG5 8RW   0602-263331

Nottingham
Stonex
197 Gladstone Street, Sherwood Rise, Nottingham NG7 6HX   0602-789050
Stone masonry.

Oxford
Symmand Company Limited
Osney Mead, Oxford OX2 0EQ   0865-249567
Specialists concerned mainly with restoring Oxford's fine buildings: woodwork,
stone and lead work.

Portsmouth
Benco and Son
29 Monmouth Road, North End, Portsmouth, Hampshire PO2 8BS   0705-64082
Specialists in renovating old property.

Ripley
Butterley Building Materials Limited
Wellington Street, Ripley, Derby DE5 3DZ   0773-43661
Bricks.

St Austell
O. E. Harford
Churchtown, St Ewe, St Austell, Cornwell PL26 6EY   072684-842391
Carpentry, joinery, masonry and electrical work.

Sheffield
H. H. Crafts
Ponds Forge, Sheaf Street, Sheffield, Yorkshire S2 5TU   0702-750123
Stained glass, cupolas, structural and decorative cast iron work, fire insets and surrounds.

Southampton
John Boston
8 Mill Close, Nursling, Southampton, Hampshire   0703-734816
Repairs and restorations of period houses.

Southampton
Southampton Yacht Services Limited
Shamrock Quay, William Street, Northam, Southampton SO1 1QL   0703-734816
Traditional joinery such as solid hardwood doors, panelling and staircases.

Southampton
W. A. Webb
13 Bellvue Road, Southampton, Hampshire SO1 2AX   0703-36525
Restoration and refurbishment of Georgian and Victorian houses.

South Peterton
Stuart Interiors and Furniture Makers
Flax Mill, Drayton, South Petherton, Somerset TA13 5LR   0460-40349

Stoke-on-Trent
John Caddick and Son Limited
Spoutfield Tileries, Staffordshire ST4 7BX   0782-616413
Ridge tiles, chimney pots and cowls.

Stoke-on-Trent
Frederick Clayton
120 Drubbery Lane, Burton, Stoke-on-Trent, Staffordshire ST3 4BT 0782-312965
Restoration of old buildings and ornamental brickwork.

Stoke-on-Trent
Daniel Platt and Sons Limited
Brownhills Tileries, Tunstall, Stoke-on-Trent, Staffordshire ST6 4NY 0782-86187
Red Crown flat quarry tiles.

Sutton Coldfield
M. S. Holden and Company
40 Coppice View Road, Sutton Coldfield B73 6UF   021-353-6075
Restoring period houses and joinery.

Swansea
Emlyn Brick Company Limited
61/62 Wind Street, Swansea SA1 1HA   0269-842247
Bricks.

Wallingford
Boschers (Cholsey) Limited
Reading Road, Cholsey, Wallingford, Oxfordshire OX10   0491-651242
Specialists in the conversion of period houses.

Weymouth
R. E. Marsh
19 Shrubbery Lane, Wyke Regis, Dorset DT4 9LY   0305-783943
Repairs, restoration and maintenance.

Wimbourne
Beacon Hill Brick Company Limited
Corfe Mullen, Wimbourne, Dorset BH21 3LY   0202-697633
Bricks.

Wimbourne
A. G. Cottrell
418 Merrifield, Couching, Wimbourne, Dorset BH21 7AJ   0202-88021
Combed reed thatching. Speciality patterned ridging and plain ridging.

Worthing
Richard A. Saulsbury
233 Ringmer Road, Worthing, West Sussex BN13 1DZ   0903-62251
Brick work, stone work and flint work renovations. Roofing and paving.

Wrexham
Dennis (Ruabon) Limited
Halfod Tileries, Ruabon, Wrexham, Clwyd LL14 6ET   0978-842283
Heather brown quarry tiles.

York
William Anelay Limited
Murton Way, Osbaldwick, York YO1 3UJ   0904-412624
Repair and conversion of historic buildings.

APPENDIX II
INSTITUTIONS AND CORPORATE BODIES OF SPECIAL INTEREST

Brick Development Association
Woodside House, Winkfield, Windsor, Berkshire SL4 2DX   0344-88651

British Flue and Chimney Manufacturers Association
Nicholson House, High Street, Maidenhead, Berks SL6 1LF   0628-34667

British Gas Corporation
152 Grosvenor Road, London SW1   01-821-1444

British Lead Manufacturers Association
68 High Street, Weybridge, Surrey KT13 8BL   97-56621

British Security Industry Association
68 St James's Street, London SW1A 1PM   01-493-6634

British Standards Institution
2 Park Street, London W1A 2BS   01-629-9000

British Wood Preserving Association
Premier House, 150 Southampton Row, London WC1 5AL   01-827-8217

Building Centre, Bristol
Stonebridge House, Colston Avenue, The Centre, Bristol BS1 4TW 0272-277002

Building Centre, London
Store Street, London WC1   01-637-1022

Building Centre, Manchester
113-115 Portland Street, Manchester M1 6FB   061-236-9802

Building Centre, Scotland
3 Claremount Terrace, Glasgow G3 7PF — 041-332-7399

Building Conservation — Trust
Apartment 39, Hampton Court Palace, East Molsey, Surrey KT8 9BS 01-943-2277

Building Regulations Division, Department of the Environment
Romney House, 43 Marsham Street, London SW1P 3PY — 01-212-3434

Building Research Advisory Service
Bucknalls Lane, Garston, Watford, Herts WD2 7JR — 0925-676612

Building Research Station
Bucknalls Lane, Garston, Watford, Herts WD2 7JR — 0925-674040

Building Research Station — Scottish Establishment
Scottish Laboratories, Kelvin Road, East Kilbride, Glasgow G75 0RZ
035-52-33941

Building Trades Journal
100 Avenue Road, London NW3 3TP — 01-935-6611

Calcium Silicate Brick Association
24 Fearnley Road, Welwyn Garden City, Herts AL8 6HW — 0707-324538

Cement and Concrete Association
Wexham Springs, Slough SL3 6PL — 028-16-2727

Cement Makers Federation
Terminal House, 52 Grosvenor Gardens, London SW1W 0AH — 01-730-2148

Civil Engineering Laboratories
RAF Cardington, Bedford MK42 0TG — 0234-58651

Civic Trust
17 Carlton House Terrace, London SW1Y 5AW — 01-930-0914

Clay Roofing Tile Council
Federation House, Station Road, Stoke-on-Trent ST4 2TJ — 0782-416256

Concrete Brick Manufacturers Association
60 Charles Street, Leicester LE1 1FB — 0533-536161

Concrete Block Association
60 Charles Street, Leicester LE1 1FB — 0533-536161

Concrete Lintel Association
60 Charles Street, Leicester LE1 1FB — 0533-536161

Concrete Society
Devon House, 12-15 Dartmouth Street, London SW1H 9BL

Copper Development Association
Orchard House, Mutton Lane, Potters Bar, Herts EN6 3AD   77-50711

Council for Small Industries in Rural Areas
Salisbury, Wiltshire SP1 3TP   0722-336255

Countryside Commission
John Dower House, Crescent Place, Cheltenham, Gloucestershire GL50 3RA
0242-521381

Department of the Environment
2 Marsham Street, London SW1P 3EB   01-212-3434

Design Council
28 Haymarket, London SW1 4SU   01-839-8000

Draught Proofing Advisory Association
P O Box 12, Haslemere, Surrey GU27 3AN   0428-54811

Electricity Council
30 Millbank, London SW1P 4RD   01-834-2333

English Heritage (Historic Building and Monuments Commission)
Fortress House, 25 Saville Row, London W1X 2BT   01-734-6010

Farm Buildings Information Centre
National Agricultural Centre, Stoneleigh, Kenilworth, Warwickshire CV8 2LG
0203-22345

Federation of Master Builders
33 John Street, London WC1   01-242-7583

Fibre Cement Manufacturers Association
PO Box 92, Elmswell, Bury St Edmunds, Suffolk IP30 9HS   0359-40963

Fire Research Station
Boreham Wood, Herts WD6 2BL   01-953-6177

Glass Manufacturers Federation
19 Portland Place, London W1N 4BH   01-580-6952

Guild of Architectural Ironmongers
8 Stepney Green, London E1 3JY   01-790-3436

Guild of Bricklayers
1 Tamhouse, Orton Malborne, Peterborough, Cambs PE2 0NA   0733-231594

Historic Buildings and Monuments Commission of English Heritage
See English Heritage

Housing Centre Trust
33 Alfred Place, London WC1E 7JU   01-637-4202

Institute of Carpenters
45 Sheen Lane, London SW14 8AB   01-876-4415

Institute of Clay Technology
C/O Butterley Building Materials, Wellington Street, Ripley, Derby DE5 3DE
                                                                  0773-43661

Institute of Wood Science
Premier House, 150 Southampton Row, London WC1B 5AL   01-837-8219

Interbuild
Building Trades Exhbition Limited, 11 Manchester Square, London W1
                                                                  01-486 1951

Land Registry
32 Lincoln's Inn Fields, London WC2A 3PH   01-405-3488

London Stove Centre
49 Chiltern Street, London W1   01-486-5168

Museum of Chimney Pots
8 Percy Street, Blandford, Dorset DT11   0258-52290

National Association of Scaffolding Contractors
82 New Cavendish Street, London W1M 8AD   01-580-5588

National Clayware Federation
7 Catle Street, Bridgwater, Somerset TA6 3DT   0278-458251

National Federation of Clay Industries
Federation House, Station Road, Stoke-on-Trent ST4 2TJ   0782-416256

National Federation of Terrazzo-Mosaic Specialists
Dickens House, 15 Tooks Court, Cursitor Street, London EC4A 1LA 01-831-7581

National Fireplace Council (Manufacturers Association)
PO Box 35, Stone on Trent ST4 2TJ   0782-44311

National Home Improvement Council
26 Store Street, London WC1E 7BT   01-636-2562

National House Building Council
58 Portland Place, London W1   01-637-1248

Northern Counties Building Information Centre
Green Lane, Old Alvet, Durham City, Co Durham DH1 3JY   0385-62611

Princes Risborough Laboratory
Princes Risborough, Aylesbury, Bucks HP17 9PX   084-44-3101

RIBA Services Limited
66 Portland Place, London W1N 4AD   01-580-5533

Royal Institute of British Architects
66 Portland Place, London W1N 4AD   01-580-5533

Sand and Gravel Association
32-36 Fleet Lane, London EC4M 4YA   01-236-0224

Scottish Office
New St. Andrews House, St James Centre, Edinburgh EH1 3SX   031-556-8400

Society of British Gas Industries
36 Holly Walk, Leamington Spa, Warwick CV32 4LY   0926-34357

Solid Fuel Advisory Service
Hobart House, Grosvenor Place, London SW1X 7AE   01-235-2020

Stone Federation
82 New Cavendish Street, London W1M 8AD   01-580-5588

Timber Research and Development Association
Stocking Lane, Hughenden Valley, High Wycombe, Bucks HP14 4ND
          0240-24-3091

Timber Trade Federation
Clareville House, Whitcomb Street, London WC2H 7DL   01-839-1891

Wood Burning Association of Retailers and Manufacturers
PO Box 35, Stoke on Trent ST4 7NU   0782-44311

APPENDIX III
GLOSSARY

A

Abutment
1. Junction where two building surfaces join. 2. Lateral support at the end of an arch or bridge. 3. Unit of solid masonry supporting an arch.

Acanthus
In classical architecture a reproduction of the leaf of this plant was frequently used as a stylish motif for decorating the capitals of Corinthian columns, arabesques, consols and cornices. Services of a skilled stonemason are required when classical features so decorated need restoring.

Acoustics
Appertaining to sound heard in a building as affected by its structure and materials of its sound reflecting surfaces. May be improved by acoustic tiles, acoustic plaster, glass wool panels and other sound absorbing materials to reduce sound bounce-back.

Adzed
Before the invention of the plane timber used in buildings was finished with an adze. Today when period houses have to be restored attempts to reproduce adzed finishes to new timbers meet with varying degrees of success.

Aggregate
Mineral particles such as stones, chippings, gravel etc, mixed with sand and cement to form concrete. For building block aggregate may consist of pumice, clinker or slag from blast furnaces.

Alcove
A recess, usually vaulted, opening out of a room or corridor.

Anaglyph
Ornament carved in low relief.

Ancone
S-shaped scrolled brackets supporting moulded features over doors, windows and fireplaces used in classical architecture. Considerable skill is needed for successful repair and restoration.

Angle bead
Wooden dowels used at external angles of walls to enable the plaster to be struck off accurately.

Angle tie
Timber used to secure the wall plates at the corners of a house with a hipped roof. Usually a dragon beam in tenoned to it.

Anthemion
Stylised decorative motif of honey-suckle.

Anti-siphonage pipe
Ventilation pipe which was developed for use where two or more pipes discharged into a common soil pipe. Located on the discharging side of the water seals of the branch pipes the function of the anti-siphonage pipe was to prevent the breakage of the seal by an extra powerful discharge from any of the branch pipes.

Arabesque
Decoration depicting leaves and plant tendrils entwined together.

Arcading
Arcades formed by several arches intended for decorative effect in Romanesque architecture.

Arch
Self supporting structure capable of carrying a load spanning an opening. Usually of bricks or stone blocks, the latter being wedge shaped to prevent slipping.

Architrave
Moulding in plaster or wood around the head and sides of doors or windows. Covers the joint between the frame and wall. An architrave around an arch is known as an archivolt. The term architrave is sometimes used to refer to a masonry framed window or doorway.

Arcuated
Constructed on series of arches.

Armature
Used for fastening the larger and heavier figures and motifs in plaster work.

Arris
Sharp corners where two surfaces meet. In most cases it may be desirable to remove the arris so that the sharp edges are less pronounced.

Art nouveau
Form of decoration started in the last twenty or so years of the 19th century which remained popular up to the First World War. In European architecture art nouveau featured flowing ornament inspired by the shapes of plants. Of recent years some attempts have been made to revive art nouveau in the graphic arts rather than in architecture.

Ashlar
1. Dressed stone for facing. 2. Very accurately cut stone permitting very thin joints. 3. Smooth masonry facings laid in regular courses. More applicable to mansions and public buildings than to more modest houses.

Ashlaring
Timber framing whose vertical members reach to the common rafters

Asphalt
Material consisting of crushed limestone and bitumen used for flooring and roofing in some cases and more extensively for paving.

Astragal
Small rounded or semi-circular moulding; may be ornamented with a reel or bead.

Astylar
A Renaissance facade without columns.

Asymmetry
Opposite of symmetry. In architectural terms asymmetry may indicate a lack of balance either in the facade or plan; this may not necessarily be displeasing.

Atlantes
Male figures supporting a classical entablature.

Attic
Room in roof of house with dormer window/s or skylights.

B

Balcony
Railed platform projecting from upper storey of house. An access balcony provides a means of entry to a number of flats in a multi-storey building.

Ball flower
Decorative flower carved as decoration at intervals along a moulding associated with the English Decorated Gothic period.

Baluster
Pillar (usually carved) for a handrail: may be wood, metal or stone. Designed as a safety measure for staircases and landings. Collectively the assembly of balusters,

newels and the handrail is known as a balustrade. Banister is another name for a baluster.

Bar
1. Steel reinforcing in concrete. 2. Intermediate member of a sash dividing individual panes of glass. 3. An arch bar may be used as a support under a brick arch. 4. Support for brickwork or stone across a fireplace opening.

Barge board
Inclined timber covering the ends of roof timbers on the gable of a house roof which is fixed just below the verge slates or tiles. Barge boards may be carved but, besides being decorative, their function is to protect the ends of the ridge board, purlins and wall plates.

Baroque
A bold, somewhat florid style of architectural decoration making considerable use of curves. The Baroque originated in Italy during the Renaissance around 1600 and exerted some influence on architecture in this country in some period buildings.

Barrel vaulting
Arched vault, the arches being semi-circular.

Base
The first (lowest) course of brickwork or masonry in a house.

Basement
A storey below the ground floor.

Basket grate
Free standing iron basket set in fireplace alcove for burning logs and perhaps large coal.

Battens
Lengths of timber used horizontally for carrying tiles, laths for plastering and for other purposes where horizontal members are needed. Also battens may be used vertically for doors, especially cottage doors and outhouse doors.

Batter
Term applied to the slight inward slope of a wall usually beginning at the base. When batter is employed the object is likely to be to strengthen the base which may be thicker than the rest of the wall.

Baulk
Squared beam of timber, usually large.

Bay
1. Window projecting from wall. 2. A division of an interior wall or a facade in which case the bay is between windows or pillars.

Bayleaf garland
Convex friezes and ceilings may be decorated with these motifs which usually depict bunches of bay leaves garlanded with ribbon.

Bay-window
Window with roof and sides protruding from wall. Not to be confused with a curved bow window.

Beam
Structural timber intended to carry a load. Traditionally a tree trunk cut to squared or rectangular cross section. Today beams may also be of reinforced concrete or steel. The usual function of beams is to support floor joists or to act as a tie for the feet of roof rafters thereby acting as roof trusses.

Bearer
Support for shelf, wall mounted cupboard, etc, when positioned horizontally.

Bed
Relating to masonry a bed may refer to a layer of stone in a quarry or the angle at which stone lies. In building a bed may refer to a bedding or base of cement mortar in which bricks are set above the concrete foundations.

Bed moulding
Moulding beneath a decorative projection such as may occur on a classical cornice.

Belfast sink
Stoneware sink shaped like a trough found in old fashioned kitchens and now in demand for miniature gardens.

Bell flower
Floral motif used to enrich convex mouldings.

Bevel
With the edge of stone or timber removed so that it slants at either more or less than 45° is to bevel it, but a cut of 45° is a chamfer.

Bill of quantities
Description of materials and work required for a given building project compiled by quantity surveyor who "takes off" information from plans and working drawings. The preparation of the bills of quantity is known as "working up". Today much of the work is done with the aid of computers.

Binder
1. Spline to hold thatch in position. 2. Member supporting ends of floor joists. 3. Binder leads are strips of lead for lead glazed lights, the cames being soldered to them.

Birds-mouth
Joint for a rafter to rest on a wall plate.

Bitumen
Term applies to any of several viscous or solid mixtures of hydrocarbons and their nitrogen and sulphur derivatives such as asphalt from Trinidad; tar residue from the distillation of coal; mineral pitch.

Blade
Main rafter in roof truss.

Blinding
1. Sand applied to hardcore to fill voids and compact it. 2. Sharp sand used with bituminous vertical dampcourse to provide key for plastering.

Block
One particular building in a complex of several buildings.

Blockboard
Material consisting of a core of laminated strips of wood or compressed wood chips faced on both sides with thin layers of wood.

Blocking course
Course of bricks or stone above a cornice.

Boasting
Removing surplus stone before carving.

Bolsection moulding
Sometimes used around door panels, wall panels and fireplaces; the moulding stands proud of the frame and may be shaped ogee or double curved.

Bond
Positioning building units such as bricks so that they interlock. Well known brick bonds include English, Flemish, Garden Wall, etc.

Bonder
Horizontal timbers built into many old brick or stone walls with the object of affording extra strength. Unfortunately such timbers sometimes rot thereby creating difficult repair jobs.

Bonnet tiles
Tiles specially shaped to cover the hips of roofs.

Boot lintel
Concrete lintel incorporated into structure so that only part of its depth is visible.

Borrowed light
Glazed opening in internal wall to allow light from one room to reach another; frequently used in walls of corridors.

Boss
A covering for the intersection of beams and ceiling ribs; usually a block either carved or moulded used at the intersections of a vaulted roof.

Bottle glass
Originally the pane of glass from which the disc was broken off from the blow pipe when glass was hand blown. Today these panes are much in demand for period houses. Also termed Crown glass.

Bow window
Curved projecting window — not to be confused with a bay window.

Brace
In timber frame construction a brace is a timber used diagonally with horizontal and vertical members to strengthen the construction.

Bracket
Support projecting from a wall to support something such as a cornice or window sill when it may be termed a console or modillion. In large constructions a bracket is often referred to as a cantilever.

Break
In building terms this denotes a change in the direction of a surface such as a wall etc.

Breast
A breast or chimney breast is the projection into a room containing the flues and fireplace/s of an internal chimney. If an external chimney is used the fireplace opening may be known as "hole in the wall."

Bressumer
Structural lintel spanning a wide opening; sometimes supporting a timber framed jetty built with cantilevered joists which are morticed and tenoned into it.

Brick
Rectangular block of baked clay or of calcium silicate. Bricks of several different kinds are available— often of different sizes. However the standard size is normally 9 inches x 4½ inches x 3 inches. Special shapes are also available. See companion volume in this series entitled Bricks and Brickwork.

Brise-soleil
A screen (usually adjustable) to reduce glare on windows. Venetian blinds serve much the same purpose.

Building block
Block made from concrete using aggregate such as coke breeze, clay or plaster for interior curtain walls.

Building by-Laws
Regulations to enable local authorities to exercise measure of control over buildings.

Bun finial
Bun shaped ornament atop a newel post at the top or bottom of a staircase handrail.

Bungalow
Single storey domestic building.

Butt hinge
Hinge sunk into edge of door or casement.

Buttress
Brick or stone support for wall, especially in the case where the outward pressure of a valuted roof needs to be resisted.

Byzantine
Appertaining to the type of architectural design and decoration in the Constantinople of the 5th century. The Byzantine influence has affected architectural design for several ages.

C

Cable mouldings
Moulding designed to look like twisted rope associated with Norman and Romanesque architecture.

Cabled fluting
Plaster fluting in which the lower part of each flute carries a convex moulding.

Camber
A surface with a slight curve raising it at the middle. The soffit of an arch may be cambered and so may the profile of a road. Without this a flat horizontal surface may appear to sag. In the case of the road the camber assists drainage of rail water. In domestic property it might be an advantage to build a car-washing area in front of a garage with a slight camber.

Cambered collar
Means of joining two rafters, the collar takes a slightly curved form so that it resembles a slightly curved arch. Lintels may be slightly cambered.

Cames
Strips of lead to hold panes of glass in lead-glazed windows.

Camp ceiling
A ceiling conforming to the configuration of the rafters at the sides and flat in the middle. Usually found in attics.

Canopy
1. Roof projecting over an entrance or pavement. 2. Roof over a window or niche.

Cantilever
Element projected from a wall and so held at only one end. A cantilevered member must depend on its own strength and the loading applied to the end by which it is held.

Capital
Moulded feature crowning a column. Each of the Roman orders had a distinctive style of capital.

Caracole
Curved outward projection of a wall — usually to house a newel staircase.

Carriage piece
Bearer to strengthen wooden steps in the middle of the flight.

Cartouche
1. Richly framed convex lozenge in the Baroque tradition. 2. Ornamental tablet designed to represent a scroll of paper. Usually has heraldric device or an inscription.

Caryatids
Female figures supporting an entablature.

Casement
Side hung window opening on its hinges. In the UK such windows open outwards; in some other countries they open inwards.

Cast iron work
Made by casting molten metal into a mould.

Cavetto
A moulding curving inwards — often in a quarter circle.

Cavity wall
Wall constructed in two leaves to prevent dampness penetrating the house or building. With standard size bricks cavity walls are usually 11 inches thick, i.e., two thicknesses of brick at 4½ inches each and a 2 inch cavity. Metal ties bridge the gap between the two leaves at intervals to give the wall strength. These ties should be furnished with a projection in their middles and used with such projections pointing downwards so that any moisture coming from the outer leaf drips downwards into the cavity and does not reach the inner leaf.

Cement
Used to bind bricks and masonry with the addition of sand and sometimes lime. Cement can be made in several ways but it usually contains chalk or limestone, clay and some gypsum.

Central heating
System of heating a house or other building from a central point at which a boiler heats water which is pumped around a circuit to radiators. In the past gravity circuits, rather than pumped circuits were popular but these entailed the use of pipes of relatively large diameter. Today's smaller pipes offer greater resistance to the passage of water so that modern systems can no longer rely on the difference between the weight of hot and cool water to create circulation without the assistance of a pump.

Centring
Temporary supports used when building brick or stone arches and vaulted ceilings and roofs.

Cess pit
Underground waterproof storage tanks used in connection with foul drains to retain sewage which must be pumped out and removed at intervals. Mainly used in country districts without main drainage.

Chain rail
Moulding running around a room at a height to prevent damage by chair backs.

Chamfer
Bevelled corners to wood or stone members to remove the arris. Beams and lintels were usually chamfered during the 17th century and earlier, especially when ceilings and openings were low.

Channel pipe
Half section pipe laid in floors likely to get wet to drain water. Useful in garages where cars are washed and in stables and outhouses.

Chase
Cutting a groove or channel in a wall or floor usually to take pipes or wiring.

Chevron
Popular decorative motif handed down from Norman architecture.

Chimney crane
Braced iron bar hinged to side of open hearth capable of being swung across the fire so that cooking pots can be suspended in the heat. Usually found in old century houses and cottages and thus in demand for old property being renervated.

Chinoiserie
Chinese type decoration featuring pagodas, timber bridges, dragons and exotic animals and birds found in houses built in the 17th and 18th Centuries.

Cladding
Sheathing a structure with a variety of materials such as brick, stone, tiles or slates etc.

Clapboarding
Boards laid horizontally so that they overlap like the planking of a carvel-built hull of a boat. Shiplap (board with a special cross section profile) makes a pleasing form of cladding for a shed, summerhouse or similar building.

Clasped purlin
Where a clasped purlin joins the main rafter it is supported by the collar of each truss.

Classical
Style of architecture originated in Ancient Greece and Rome and revived in the Renaissance.

Clerestory
Upper storey of a house above the other parts of the building.

Clerk of works
One who inspects the progress of the building operation on behalf of the architect and makes sure the quality of the materials and workmanship is satisfactory.

Cloam oven
Old fashioned earthenware oven built into wall near the hearth (or in the hearth itself) sometimes found in period houses and cottages. On baking days the oven was heated with suitable fuel which was then removed, the dough was then put inside and the door sealed with clay to enable the dough to cook. A feature beloved by enthusiasts for restoring old cottages.

Closed ring staircase
Staircase in which the ends of the treads are housed in the strings, in contrast to an open string staircase where the shape of the stairs is cut out of the strings so that the treads rest on them. The wall string is fixed to the wall of the stairwell.

Clout nail
Term usually refers to a fairly short galvanised nail with a large head.

Cluster block
A house or building having, on plan, several wings which are connected to it.

Coach bolt
Round headed bolt with a square shank.

Coach screw
A strong screw with a square bolt head; mainly for securing steel plates to timbers.

Cob
Mixture of mud and binding materials such as hair used as an infill for walling.

Cock's head hinges
"H" hinges of brass or iron found in 17th Century houses.

Coffers
Recessed panels sometimes found in old ceilings, volts and occasionally in domes.

Collar beam
Feature of roof construction common in houses built before the war. The beam runs horizontally across the main rafters of a roof truss and is usually as thick as these rafters to which it is usually morticed and tenoned. Thus the rafters are securely jointed between the wall plate and the ridge board.

Collars
Horizontal timbers attached to pairs of rafters preventing the ends of the rafters coming apart under strain. Ceilings of attics are usually fixed to collar purlins which may sometimes be supported by crown posts. Other collars are relatively short timbers keeping rafters together near the apex.

Colonial
The architecture of the early English colonies of New England. In the southern American states the style gained considerable popularity and followed the Georgian tradition.

Composite order
Classical order which attempted to combine the Ionic capital with the Corinthian capital. In this style the scrolls of the Ionic order were retained but they were combined with the acanthus foliage of the Corinthian order.

Composition concrete tiles
Tiles produced from fine textured concrete, sometimes coloured — usually interlocking.

Concrete
Mixture of cement, sand, water and aggregate which sets hard.

Conduit
Protective casing for electrical cables and wiring.

Console
Timber, stone or plaster bracket often in the form of an S scroll. Alternative name: ancones. Usually employed to carry higher parts of a cornice.

Continued chimneypiece
Large chimney extending high above the building and having a bold cornice or pediment.

Coping
Brick or stone capping to a wall. Sometimes used to top a gable wall.

Corbel
Projecting bracket. Alternatively a timber or stone projection from a wall to carry a

load such as a structural beam. Some corbels are richly carved. A corbel table relates to a unit at the eaves featuring a miniature arcade.

Core
Interior of a wall constructed of masonry, usually on both faces.

Corinthian order
Classical order of architecture using columns with capitals decorated with acanthus leaves. Popular with the Romans and into the Renaissance.

Cornice
Projecting upper part of the entablature in classical and Renaissance architecture.

Corona
Flat middle area of cornice.

Counter battens
Usually nailed to battens running in the opposite direction to provide plenty of fixing points for boards or laths.

Counter lathing
Laths set under a collection of laths to raise these laths.

Couple
Pair of rafters without a ridgeboard. Commonly found in mediaeval houses and in some modern houses.

Course
Horizontal layer of bricks or stones.

Cove
Used like a cornice to join walls to ceilings.

Cradling
Timber bracket supporting ornamental plasterwork or elaborate cornice.

Cramp
Metal tie piece used to hold stonework together in masonry.

Crazing
Hair cracks in rendering. Not necessarily serious.

Creasing course
Two layers of tiles in a wall, generally under the coping.

Crenellation
Indentation in upper part of parapet. Commonly found in castles and occasionally in modern houses. In medieval times crenellation required the permission of the

sovereign because it could protect the archers loyal to the castle's owner.

Crocket
Projecting block used in Gothic architecture usually heavily carved to decorate spires and canopies.

Cross wall
Walls designed to relieve external walls of heavy loads.

Crown glass
Panes of glass at the centre of the glass blower's disc having a distinctive marking where the molten glass was cut off.

Crown posts
When trusses consist of pairs of rafters joined by tie beams crown posts and collar purlins were often used to support the roof structure.

Cupola
Hemispherical roof.

Curtail step
Lowest step of a staircase which curls around like a cur's tail.

Cusp
Carved projection between the lobes of a Gothic arch. Also a tooth separating foliations of tracery windows.

D

Dado
Lower part of interior wall decorated differently from the remainder of the wall. The dado may be between 2ft 6in and 4ft 6ins high.

Damp course
Layer of slate, lead or bitumen or special damp proof felting placed in a wall to guard against dampness migrating upwards.

Damp proof membrane
Usually takes the form of a plastic sheet laid over hardcore or other sub-floor before a solid floor is laid.

Decastyle
Row of ten columns.

Decorated
English Gothic architecture during more or less the 14th century.

Dentil
Projection from a cornice which looks like the end of a rafter.

Die
Used to form a section for making cames from lead.

Die
In joinery the square section blocks of turned baluster fixed to the handrail and the string or tread.

Diminishing courses
Roof tiles set out so that, from eaves to ridge, each row of tiles show less of the tiles than the preceding row. Thus the lap of each row of tiles over the row beneath increases nearer the ridge.

Distress
Staining, scoring, denting and marking etc. materials to make them look old. Replacing old beams with modern timbers presents an opportunity for carrying out this exercise.

Dog grate
Iron or steel basket grate for fire which is free standing and may incorporate a fireback.

Dog leg staircase
The first flight leads to a half landing and the second flight then doubles back.

Dome
A roof of hemispherical shape.

Doorcase
The joinery surrounding a door opening.

Doorhood
Projection over a doorway to enhance its appearance and afford protection from the weather.

Doric order
Simplest and least ornate of the three architectural orders of Ancient Greece.

Dormer
Window projecting from roof.

Dosseret
Block above a Byzantine capital when an arch has wide voussiors.

Dovetail
Joining two pieces of timber (usually when used at right angles to each other) by means of cutting out wedge-shaped portions of each.

Masonry dowel
Small slate or metal peg for joining pieces of stone.

Down hearth
Fireplace where the fire rests on bed of ashes and no grate is used although firedogs may be employed.

Dressing
Outside a house other than plain work, such as sills, ashlar quoins etc in brick or rubble. Alternatively well cut and finished stonework often at the opening in a wall.

Dripstone
Used mainly in Gothic architecture — a projecting stone, usually carved, above a doorway to conduct rainwater away from where it is not wanted.

Drum
Cylindrical lower part of a dome or cupola, sometimes with windows to admit light.

Dry rot
Decay in wood caused by a fungus.

Dubbing
Filling cavities in wall prior to plastering.

Duck's nest grate
Similar to a hob grate, but generally lower.

E

Early English
13th Century English Gothic architecture during which lancet windows were popular.

Eaves
That part of a roof which overhangs the wall.

Edwardian
Architectural style during the reign of Edward VII; 1901-1910.

Efflorescence
Crystalline deposit which appears on walls due to the presence of salts in the wall. Usually occurs as a new wall dries out.

Egg and dart moulding
Small ornamental mouldings said to resemble eggs and darts.

Elevation
Drawing depicting the geometrical projection of a building on a plane perpendicular to the horizon.

Elizabethan
English early Rennaissance architecture about the time of Queen Elizabeth I.

Empire style
Early 19th Century architectural style showing an Egyptian influence but with some regard to neo-classical forms.

Encaustic tiles
Earthenware tiles, usually glazed and well patterned used extensively during the Victorian and Edwardian periods.

English bond
Brickwork laid in alternative courses of headers and stretchers.

Entablature
Upper element of the classical order consisting of the cornice, frieze and, below these, the architrave.

Entasis
Slight convex tapering of a column so that it does not appear to curve inwards.

Escutcheon
Swivelling plate covering the keyhole of a door.

F

Facade
The elevation (principal front) of a house or other building.

Face bedding
Stone set with its natural bed on edge.

Fairface
Well executed brick or stonework with good pointing may be described as being "fairfaced."

Fall
Slope in a flat roof for draining water.

Fanlight
Window over a doorway — fan shaped where there is an arch over the doorway; otherwise fanlights may be oblong.

Fascia
Plain band of small projection used horizontally either in the entablature or elsewhere. Classical Architraves may contain more than one of these bands.

Felt
Bituminous felt has two principal uses in building: 1. Damp courses; 2. Roofing.

Fielded panel
Door panel or wall panel with a centre proud of its framework, its edges being

sloped (fielded) off and inserted in a groove in the framing.

Fillet
Thin strip of wood or plaster. In masonry fillets are sometimes used between more elaborate mouldings.

Finial
Ornament at the apex of a gable. Also used to decorate staircase newel posts.

Fireback
Cast iron screen placed at the back of the hearth to protect the rear of the fireplace opening and to reflect heat into the room. Believed to have become popular during the 16th Century. Used throughout the 17th Century and later.

Firrings
Tapered lengths of timber fixed to the upper part of joists of a flat roof to ensure the fall required for surface drainage.

Fishplates
Steel plates bolted either side of joins of timber when the latter are joined end to end.

Fishtail
Splitting and slightly opening the end of a metal cramp to afford a better grip when set in cement.

Flamboyant
In France the last phase of Gothic architecture at about the time of the Perpendicular and Decorated periods were going on in England. The Flamboyant style is characterized by ornate carving and elaborate tracery.

Flange
Plates at the top and bottom of an I section steel joist. The vertical plane section joining the horizontal plane flanges is the web.

Flashings
Lead or other water-proof material used around the abutments between roof slates or tiles and chimneys and around window and door openings. Copper, zinc and — these days — aluminium may also be used as flashings. Occasionally cement flashings are encountered.

Flaunching
Domed capping of mortar around the base of a chimney pot to secure it to the stack and to throw off rain and snow.

Fleche
Slender spire rising from a roof.

Flemish bond
Bricks laid with headers and stretchers alternately in each course.

Flitch-plate
Steel member set along the middle of a beam's face or between sections of a composite beam to impart additional strength.

Float
Tool used for applying plaster and for rendering.

Floating
Second coat applied in 3-coat plastering.

Flue
Shaft of a chimney.

Flush door
Door with the surface of each side on one plane as distinct from a panelled door.

Flushwork
Decoration for wall with stone panelling and an infilling of knapped flints.

Fluting
Parallel concave channels decorating a column, pilaster or architrove.

Flying buttress
Masonry used in a form resembling a segment of an arch taking the thrust of a vault or roof to a buttress.

Foil
Arc shaped opening between the cusps in tracery.

Footing
Widening at the base of a wall to provide large area for bearing.

Footing
The base of a wall, usually thicker than the rest of the wall to distribute the load over a wider area.

Formwork
Wooden casing in which concrete may be moulded.

Foundations
Base of structure extending to below the level of the surrounding ground and extended to support load.

Frame construction
Method of building enabling roof and floors to be supported on a frame. Earlier

examples were timber framed houses. Between the frame's members the walls are not load bearing although they must keep out the weather.

Freestone
Stone which can be tooled for masonry building. Term relates particularly to fine grained stone which can be worked in any direction such as most limestone or sandstone.

French windows
Pair of glazed doors giving access to outside — usually the garden. Originally they opened inwards like windows in France. Today many so called "French windows" in this country open outwards.

Fresco
Wall painting done while plaster is wet. Not painted in oils.

Fret
Commonly found in Renaissance architecture. Small bands (fillets) interlacing where they cross at right angles.

Frieze
Decorative design at or near the top of the wall but in classical architecture the middle element of three which constitute an entablature so that the frieze is between the architrave and the cornice.

Frog
Hollowed out area of a brick to reduce its weight and provide key for a good bed of mortar.

Functionalism
Architectural design which paid special attention to considerations of fitness to purpose. Also exploiting the characteristics of the building site to the best possible advantage.

G

Gable
Wall of house or building which is triangular at the top section to conform to the pitch of the roof.

Gang boards
Boarding over ceiling joists to form a floor in a loft.

Gauge
1. Distance between the top of one batten to take roof slates and the top of the batten below it. This determines the distance from the tail of one slate to the tail of the slate below it. The latter is termed the margin. 2. Measurement of thickness of sheet metal, wire and screws. 3. Mesh sizes of sieves for gauging aggregate. 4. When

mixes of plaster or mortar contain both cement and lime as well as sand they are "gauged".

Geometric staircase
Generally cantilevered from central pillar or, in some cases, an open well. Usually circular on plan so that it makes economical use of space on plan.

Georgian
English Renaissance architecture from George I to George IV.

Gesso
Gypsum or chalk mixed with glue used as a dense white base for decorative purpose. Unlikely to withstand damp conditions successfully.

Gilding
Metallic leaf—usually gold—applied with gold size. Costly but lasts well under the right conditions.

Girder
Metal beam. Lattice beams are constructed of several small beams to provide as much strength as possible consistent with their weight. Girders are used as principal horizontal members in frame structures.

Glass
Non-crystalline material available for building purposes in sheet form which is made by fusing silica (sand) with soda or potash. Lead oxide may also be added. Available in several forms for building, including toughened glass, block glass, heat resisting glass, clear glass for windows and obscured glass etc.

Glazing bars
Wooden framing members in a window sash. In general 17th Century glazing bars were usually thick and clumsy: thinner and better in the 18th Century and thinner still and more elegant in the next century. Even quite early in the 19th Century glazing bars were very thin and graceful besides admitting more light and affording a better view from windows.

Going
Width of stairtread from front to back less the projecting nosing.

Gothic
The style of architecture popular in England and most of Europe from the 13th to the 16th Century. Considerable use was made of pointed arches and pointed windows. What is known as the Gothic Revival occurred during the late 18th and early 19th Centuries. Early during the revival period what became known as 'Strawberry Hill Gothic' became popular.

Graining
The art of staining and painting softwoods to resemble hardwoods with attractive

figuring. Less common today but enjoyed great popularity before and after the First World War, especially in London's public houses. Good graining requires considerable skill and experience.

Grid
Layout of the principal members of a structure.

Grillage
Foundation making use of two or more layers of rolled steel joists embedded in concrete slab.

Grip handrail
Elizabethan or Jacobean handrail, often with a roll moulding. A substantially constructed job.

Groin
Angluar curve created by two arches intersecting in vaulting.

Grounds
Rough timber fixings plugged or otherwise secured to walls, ceilings and floors to provide fixings for joinery.

Grout
Thin mortar used as a filling. Grout may be used in a slightly thicker form to consolidate walls before they are rendered.

Gudgeon
Design consisting of interlacing circles.

Gudgeon pin
A round pin (of mild steel) atached to a backplate to which a strap hinge may be socketed.

Gully
Cast iron or salt glazed ware receptacle above a drain.

Gully trap
A U-bend water seal at the top of a drain to stop gases escaping.

Guttae
Ornaments positioned beneath the triglyphs and mutules of a typical entablature of the Doric order. Usually more or less cone shaped.

H

Habitable rooms
Building Regulations require certain stipulated standards for rooms classed as 'habitable.' Details are given in the regulations.

Half timbered
Houses constructed with timber frames and infills between the timbers. Some of the timbers may consist of two separate pieces of wood. Where these are joined by what is known as 'halved joints' half of each piece of timber being joined is cut away towards its end and the two timbers so treated may be fitted to each other for secure joining.

Hammer beam roof
Timber roof construction making use of a wooden arch instead of a tie-beam.

Hanging stile
A door's vertical member on the hinged side of the frame.

Hardboard
Double faced board with a core of compressed fibre and wood waste. Available in large sheets.

Hardcore
Broken stone, rubble and brick well rammed and used as a base for floors, pavings and paths.

Hardwood
Timber cut from broad leaved trees.

Header
Brick set in a one-brick wall (9 inches thick) with its ends showing on the faces.

Hearth
Solid slab set on the constructional hearth, both of which must be of incombustible material such as concrete or stone. The hearth should extend under the fireplace opening and into the room in accordance with the requirements of the Building Regulations.

Herring bone strutting
Criss-cross timbers tightly wedged between joists to prevent them from warping, tilting or otherwise getting out of true.

Herring bone work
Zigzag pattern formed by bricks lain diagonally in courses.

H-hinge
Hinges which were nailed rather than screwed and used in the 17th and 18th Centuries.

Hip
Angle between roof top slopes.

Hip rafter
Diagonally positioned rafter at the external junction of sloping roofs.

Hipped roof
Roof when the sides are at the same pitch forming salient sloping known as hips.

Holdfast
Steel plate, flat and tapered to a point at one end and with a hole at the wide end for a screw. Used for fastening door frames securely when it is driven into brickwork or masonry joints.

Hood moulding
Mouldings generally found above early windows.

Horn
In joinery a projection may be left on an item for fixing into the wall. Sometimes used for fastening door and window frames or may take the form of being an extension of the style of the upper sash in a sash window which is double hung. In some cases a horn may be used to strengthen the fastening of the bottom rail.

Horn sash
In some Victorian houses these are extensions of the sash styles so that the joint between the sash and rail may be a mortice and tenon.

Hydrated lime
Dry lime in the form of fine powder which has been slaked before being bagged.

Hydraulic lime
Sets by chemical reactions as well as evaporation and is sometimes preferred because it resembles Portland cement to some extent. Useful for bedding and pointing masonry.

I

Impost
The cap of a pilaster from which an arch strings.

Inglenook
Extra large fireplace recess with a down-hearth and a wide chimney opening. Often with seat/s either side. Popular in the 17th and 18th Centuries.

Inlaid floor
Type of parquet floor using strips of wood; occasionally termed marquetry flooring.

In situ
In the building trade this refers to work carried out where the unit being made will remain. A concrete lintel may, for example, be cast in situ.

Inspection chamber
A manhole at points above a drainage system to enable the drains to be inspected and cleaned. Usually situated where the direction of the drain changes.

Insulation
Use of non-heat-conducting material to retard the passing of heat through a wall, floor or ceiling.

Intarsia
Decorative inlay usually of wood.

Interlocking tiles
Tiles with edges which fit into one another to produce a reliable seal against rain.

Intrados
Inner curve of an arch. The term is sometimes used to denote the lowest course of stones or bricks in an arch.

Intumescent
Liable to swell and expand.

Invert
Lowest part of a drainpipe's interior; point at which moisture will begin to gather.

Ionic
Second of the three Greek orders which was copied by the Romans. Large volutes sometimes with scrolls but without acanthus leaves.

J

Jacobean
English Renaissance architecture which became popular early in the 17th Century during the reign of James I. The decoration was often elaborate and somewhat Gothic and sometimes showed signs of trying to capture a classical flavour.

Jamb
Vertical member of a door or window opening. Jambs may be constructed of wood, brick or stone but a wood framework is most usual.

Jetty
The overhanging part of a timber framed house supported by the ends of the joists of the first floor. Most commonly found in early timbered houses and buildings.

Jib door
A door which looks like part of the wall panelling. Sometimes used to afford entrance to a secret chamber.

Jinny wheel
Before the days of lifts for use on construction sites jinny wheels were in common use. They were pulleys slung from scaffolding and used for hauling up building materials.

Joinery
Making and fitting woodwork such as staircases, doors, windows and panelling.

Joint
Where two items are joined together. An expansion joint is a flexible joint which permits some movement between the two items jointed, usually to allow for expansion and contraction caused by temperature changes.

Joint-bedding
Stone set with its natural bed vertical.

Joists
Timbers supporting floor boards and flat roofs.

K

Key
Indented or roughened surface to obtain adhesion when plaster is applied.

Keystone
Central wedge-shaped stone or an arch.

King post
Timber running vertically from the tie beam of a roof truss to the roof ridge.

Kneeler
Stone block with an inclined face in a gable wall to carry a coping stone.

Knotting
Shellac for painting knots so that resin within them does not leak out and into paintwork.

L

Lagging
Insulating materials around cisterns and pipes.

Lancet arch
12th or 13th Centuries arch resembling a lancet.

Lancet window
Window having a sharply pointed arch popular in Early English Gothic architecture during the 13th Century.

Landing
Floor area at the top of a flight of stairs.

Lath
Thin strip of sawn wood used to support plaster, slates or tiles.

Ledged and braced door
Door with diagonal timbers fastened between ledges to brace the door.

Ledger
1 Door with horizontal boards on the inside to hold the vertical boards outside together. 2 Horizontal rods for retaining thatch.

Lewis hole
Dovetail shaped hole in a large stone for lifting it with a hooked tool.

Lierne
In Gothic vaulting — the supporting rib between two principal ribs.

Linenfold
Wood carving to represent folds of linen popular in Tudor times.

Lining
Covering rough brickwork or masonry door or window jambs. Also used for fair facing internal walls.

Lintel
Reinforced concrete beam or timber spanning aperture in wall. Must be strong enough to carry the load on it.

Listed building
Building listed by the Department of the Environment as being of particular architectural or historical interest.

Listings
Fillets along the abutment between a roof and chimney or wall. May be of mortar, tiles or slates.

Lock rail
In a panelled door the horizontal rail in which the lock is set.

Loggia
Roofed gallery, sometimes in association with an open arcade.

Louvre
An opening for ventilation fitted with sloping slats to admit air but keep out rain.

Lozenge
Diamond shaped decoration popular in the Jacobean period.

M

Maisonette
Domestic dwelling of more than one storey making up part of a house and usually consisting of two storeys.

Manhole
Inspection chamber.

Mansard Roof
Roof with steep sides and somewhat flat upper part considered to be French or Dutch in style.

Margin
The section of a tile or slate not covered by another tile or slate.

Marginal bars
Narrow glazing bars around the edge of a window light.

Marquise
Glass canopy projecting over the entrance to a house or building.

Mast newel staircase
Spiral staircase housed in a central post.

Match boards
Softwood boards, often with a beaded edge, for lining internal walls.

Mechanical bond
Structural bond as distinct from adhesion enabling two different building materials to be fastened together. Plaster pressed into expanded metal has a mechanical bond, but paint applied to a surface relies on adhesion.

Medallion
Decorative motif, usually circular or oval in shape.

Medullary rays
Radial markings which may show up on the saw cuts of timber.

Mezzanine
Storey between ground and first floors.

Mitre
Mouldings sawn at 45° so that they butt together to form a right angle.

Modillions
Decorative scrolled brackets under the corona of a classical cornice.

Modular
Houses designed and built on the modular principle using standard size modules the dimensions of which are co-ordinated by adopting standard sizes.

Module
The module was well known in classical architecture; it was half the dimension of a

column at its base and was sub divided into thirty sections called minutes. Today module refers to units of standard size the use of which reduces time needed on the building site to erect the structure.

Mortar
Plastic mix of cement and sand with, in some cases, lime. Used for bedding bricks and stone.

Mortice
Cut out of timber to take a tenon.

Mosaic
Design formed by cuboids or tesserae of coloured glass or stone to decorate floors or walls.

Moulding
Decorative curves carved on projections. Running ornaments in strip form for application as required.

Muff glass
Glass which was blown in the form of a cylinder then cut lengthways and unrolled into a flat sheet for use in windows. Not particularly easy to match when using modern glass.

Muffle
A metal template used in the early stages of producing a moulding. It is slightly oversize; unlike the template used for the final coat.

Mullion
Vertical glazing bar dividing the lights of a window. It may be of wood or stone or even cast iron. However metal mullions are somewhat unusual.

Muntin
Vertical member between the stiles in a panelled door or between wall panelling.

Muntin and planking
Vertical boards with their edges slotted into the edges of thicker members. This is sometimes known as studs.

Mutule
Inclined block projecting from a Doric Cornice.

N

Necking
A section of the Roman Doric capital between the Astragal and the capital itself.

Needle
Timber built into wall to take the thrust of other timbers.

Neo-classical
Architectural design popular in the second half of the 18th Century. Often associated with Robert Adam the architect and furniture maker.

Newel
Central pillar of a spiral staircase. Also a post where a flight of stairs changes direction or terminates at a landing. Usually of timber, but sometimes of metal or stone.

Niche
A recess in a wall, usually rounded.

Nogging
Timber supports between the verticals of partition walls in timber frame houses.

Norfolk latches
Sometimes known as Norfolk and Suffolk latches these latches have a handgrip and thumb plate one side of a door and a sneck on the other. This may be of wood or metal.

Norman
Late 11th and 12th Century architecture in England similar to Romanesque architecture on the European Continent.

Nosing
That rounded section of a stairtread projecting from the edge of the riser.

Notch
Groove in a timber to take another timber.

O

Ogee
Arch or moulding ending in a point popular in late Gothic period and inspired by Muslim architecture. The term ogee moulding may also refer to an S shaped section.

Open well stairs
A staircase consisting of short flights separated by quarter landings so that an open well is formed. Unlikely to be used in many modern houses as the form of construction requires a good deal of space.

Oriel
Bay windows on the first storey and above on brackets. Occasionally oriel windows may be projected from a wall on the ground floor but this appears to be somewhat unusual.

Overmantle
Upper section of large chimneypiece above the mantle shelf. Suitable for large rooms with lofty ceilings.

Ovolo
Convex moulding or carving associated with the Renaissance movement.

P

Palladian
Inigo Jones and the English version of Palladian architecture was based to some extent on the style of Andrea Palladio a couple of centuries earlier when the Renaissance was popular.

Pallets
Low platforms to move building materials by forklift truck. Thin softwood built into walls to provide fixing places for joinery.

Panelled spandrel
A partition to create an enclosed cupboard beneath a staircase.

Pantile
Tile with a wavy or hollow surface which is made to interlink with other similar tiles.

Parapet
Low wall extending the walls of a house above the eaves. Also the battlements of a fortress.

Pargetting
External plasterwork of a decorative nature.

Parging
Plastering the interior of a flue.

Party wall
Wall dividing two adjoining properties.

Patera
Oval or circular decoration associated with the Neo-Classical style and found in some of the work attributed to Robert Adam.

Patio
Originally a courtyard in Spanish architecture. Today the term is often used to denote a paved area outside a house, often with access through an extension.

Pavement lights
Blocks of glass set in metal or concrete frameworks for use in pavements where natural light is needed below.

Pavimentum
Decoration for a pavement consisting of coloured stone set in cement.

Pebble dash
A popular treatment for walls (especially when built of flettons) which is achieved by dashing on small pebbles or pea gravel while the cement or plaster rendering is still wet and plastic. Said to have a favourable effect on weatherproofing the wall.

Pedestal
Rectangular base for a classical column or statue.

Pediment
Triangular low gable above the entablature sometimes found in classical styles. The pediment also appears sometimes in Renaissance architecture when it may be broken or curved.

Peggies
Small slates the width of which is half or more of the depth. However the widths may vary.

Pellating
The use of wooden plugs to hide recessed screwheads. These pellets should match the colour and grain of the wood in which they are used if their purpose is to be achieved.

Penthouse
Additional structure generally on the roof of a building. Often associated in the minds of the public with the possession of wealth.

Pentice
Roof for an outside staircase.

Peripteral
Area completely surrounded by a colonnade facing outwards.

Perpendicular
Late Gothic — a style of architecture which came after the Decorated period.

Perpends
Vertical joints between bricks or masonry set in courses.

Picturesque
Term associated with both buildings and their gardens and grounds denoting a somewhat informal style sometimes adopted in the late 18th and early 19th Centuries.

Pier
A wall more or less isolated from other walling. Alternatively a vertical support for a bridge, an arch or other structure.

Pilaster
Rectangular projection for a column the design of which is determined by the order

of the architecture of which the pilaster is part.

Pile
Length of steel, reinforced concrete or even wood driven into the ground to form the basis of foundations on ground for which other kinds of foundation would be unsatisfactory. Often needed beside a river where the ground may collapse.

Pillar
Vertical support generally smaller than a pier.

Pinnacle
Masonry, often in decorative form, to provide weight at the summet of a buttress or as a finial.

Pitch
Inclination of a roof. The traditional angle varies slightly from county to county and depends mainly on the kind of roof covering used in the district. Today's interlocking tiles are capable of shedding rain even if the roof does not have a steep pitch.

Plain tile
This usually denotes an ordinary roofing tile.

Plan
Drawing of a horizontal section of a house or other building — usually at ground level but not necessarily. Plans may be needed for each storey and for the roof structure.

Plinth
Projecting base of wall or other structure which spreads weight over a larger area of ground. Columns often stand on plinths.

Plumb
Vertical and true. A plumb bob consists of bricklayer's line with a cone shaped weight on the end to determine a true vertical.

Plywood
Formed by thin layers of wood glued together with the grain of each lamination at right angles to its neighbour.

Point block
Blocks of flats of greater height than width or length. Also known as tower blocks.

Pointing
Finishing the joints in brickwork or masonry with mortar usually richer than the bedding mortar and sometimes specially coloured. There are several kinds of pointing.

Portal frame
Vertical columns or stanchions and rafters to make a framework for reinforced concrete buildings.

Poung boards
Boards lining a trench to prevent collapse of sides.

Prefabrication
System of building for which units are produced in a factory for speedy assembly on site.

Principal rafters
The very strong rafters carrying the load of the roof which usually consists of purlins, the common rafters, battens and tiles or slates.

Purlin
Longitudinal timber supporting roof trusses or the rafters. Usually timber but steel is sometimes used in large houses and buildings.

Putlog
Horizontal scaffolding which is traditionally set in a wall.

Putty
Plastic composition which sets hard when exposed to air. Composed of whiting and linseed with, in some cases, special driers. Used mainly for glazing and stopping. Lime putty, made of lime which is well slaked, is useful for plaster work. Mason's putty is a mixture of lime putty and stone dust which must be very fine since such putty is used for very thin joints in masonry.

Q

Quadrangle
An open square usually surrounded on four sides by buildings but occasionally with one side left open. Rather similar to a courtyard.

Quadrant
In building the term refers to a moulding which, in section, represents a quarter of a circle.

Quarry
Glass pane in leaded glazing — usually a small piece of glass.

Quarry tile
Clay floor tile red, buff or brown. Very hard wearing.

Quatrefoil
Opening in Gothic tracery.

Queen Anne
Domestic architecture betwen the Restoration and the Georgian periods. Mainly concerned with brick houses but also occasionally with stone buildings.

Queen posts
Vertical structural timbers between tie beams and purlins which, if supporting the collar rather than the purlin, may be termed a queen strut. Pairs of queen posts are commonly used instead of a king post as these provide less interruption to the roof space.

Quick lime
Unslaked lime. When mixed with water the lime becomes slaked and hydrated.

Quirk
V-shaped groove between two mouldings.

Quoins
Dressed stones or bricks forming corners of walls. Often quoins are alternatively long and short. If the infill is brick and the quoin stone its height may equal more than one course of brickwork.

R
Racking
Irregular end of wall which is not complete or has been broken.

Rafter
Inclined timber carrying roof covering.

Rag bolts
Strong, heavy bolts with enlarged splayed ends for burying in mortar as a wall is built.

Ragstone
Stone laid as rubble because it is too hard for tooling. Rough rubble walls are sometimes termed rag work. The term may also apply to work executed with extra large, rough slates.

Rails
Horizontal members in doors or panelling.

Raking cut
Bricks, tiles or slates cut at angles which are not right angles.

Raking shore
Inclined stay used to support a damaged wall which would otherwise be unsafe.

Ramp
Inclined path or road from one level to another. Motorists will know ramps as the

change from one level of a road surface to another.

Randoms
Slates, usually between 300 mm and 600 mm deep but of varying widths. Such slates should not be less than half as wide as their depth.

Random rubble
Term applied to walls built of irregular shaped stones of different sizes set in lime mortar, cement mortar, earth or dry-jointed. Such dry walls may have a capping of stones bedded in cement mortar. While dry stone walls are not as strong as walls built with stones and mortar they often last for years in reasonable condition because they offer less resistance to the wind which blows through their crevices so that its force is partly dissipated.

Rebate
Step-shaped recess in a timber member. Window lights which do not open are rebated to take glass.

Reeding
Achieved by the use of closely spaced round beading. Popular for 19th century architraves.

Regency
In England the architectural style popular during the reign of George IV based on classical architecture.

Register plate
Metal plate used in a fireplace opening. May be used to restrict the opening to the flue or seal it if the fire is not in use. In the latter case the chimney pot will probably need capping. If the pot is not capped adequate ventilation should be provided at the fireplace even when this is not used.

Reinforced concrete
Concrete containing steel reinforcement to give additional strength.

Relief
Figures or decorations carved in relief.

Relieving arch
In brickwork and masonry an arch may be built above a lintel or another arch to help take the weight by carrying this on the jambs.

Renaissance
Kind of architecture fashionable in Europe from the 15th to the 17th Century.

Rendering
Applying the first coat of plaster to a wall inside a house; in some circumstances this coat may be of mortar instead of plaster. Exterior surfaces of walls are normally

rendered with a mortar consisting of cement and sand. When the rendering is done on laths the material being used must be pressed into the openings between the laths. This kind of rendering is sometimes termed pricking up.

Rere arch
An arch carrying a masonry wall where the wall spans an opening.

Respond
A half pillar to terminate an arcade.

Returns
When a wall decorated with a running moulding changes direction at right angles the moulding should be continued around the return.

Reveal pin
Device enabling scaffolding to be fixed to a window. A reveal is a side of the opening in a wall needed for a window.

Rib
Term for a projecting band on a ceiling or vault.

Ribbon development
More or less continuous housing development along a stretch of main road. Prevalent during the early years following the First World War.

Ribbon pointing
Pointing which stands proud of stonework sometimes called strap pointing.

Ridge
Apex of a roof. Ridge boards run along the apex and provide a fixing for the upper ends of rafters which may be attached to a ridge purlin. Ridge tiles are either angled tiles for use at ridges or half round tiles to be used in the same position.

Rim lock
Lock with a metal case to enable it to be fastened to the surface of a door.

Riser
Vertical member of a staircase between two treads. The upper edge of the riser will help to support the tread in the middle of the step, i.e., between the two strings.

Riven
Stone of a flaky nature which is split along its laminations. Flagstones are riven.

Rococo
Late baroque period; elaborate decoration making considerable use of scrolls and shells.

Roman cement
Up the end of the 19th Century this was used extensively for preparing plaster work. Roman cement is brownish and is derived from certain clay. It sets by becoming subject to certain chemical changes as well as by evaporation.

Romanesque
In Britain this architectural style was called Roman but in Europe it was termed Romanesque. Popular between the 9th and 12th Centuries.

Roof trusses
Sloping timbers meeting the ridgeboard at the same place in the ridge and often used with a horizontal timber to complete a triangle.

Roof
Structure over a house or building supported by the walls and designed as protection against the weather.

Rosette
Stylised circular decoration based on flower motif.

Rose window
Circular shaped window with mullions converging at the centre.

Rough cast
Mixture of lime and fine aggregate thrown on wall before its plastic state sets and hardens. Used frequently as a facing where common flettons or blocks are used.

RSJ
Customary abbreviation for rolled steel joist.

Rubber
Soft unfrogged brick for shaping by sawing and rubbing often employed in flat arches.

Rubble
Stone or imperfect brick used as foundation for floors, paths or roads. Usually rammed down and often with the voids filled or partly filled with fine aggregate before cement concrete is applied. The term may also refer to stone laid at random to form a solid structure rather than with two masonry faces and a core.

S

Saddle bar
Horizontal bar used in leaded lights to retain the glazing in position.

Sarking boards
Fastened to the upper edges of rafters before applying slates or tiles. Boarded roofs provide better protection against rough weather.

Sash
Frame of window holding the glass and usually sliding up and down, being held in any position by a cord with counterweights passing over pulleys. A sash box may house the cords and counterweights. The heavier window frame in which the lighter sash frame moves up and down is often termed the sash frame. Occasionally sash windows open and close by sliding horizontally.

Saucer dome
Shallow dome in roof resembling an inverted saucer in shape.

Scaffold
Framework for temporary platforms around a building under construction. At one time scaffolding poles were of wood: today steel is commonly used, the horizontals, vertical members and any diagonals used being fastened with special clips.

Scagliola
A plaster substitute for natural marble used in the 18th Century.

Scantling
1. Length of masonry more than 6 ft long. 2. Length of timber usually 2 to 4 inches thick and up to ½ inch wider. 3. The term is sometimes used in connection with the dimensions to which timber or stone is to be cut.

Scarfing
Timber being spliced longitudinally.

Scionson arch
Arch supporting an inner face of masonry wall over an opening.

Scotia moulding
Concave moulding with a design which is not necessarily symmetrical.

Screed
Mortar (usually an inch or two thick) to level and smooth a floor. May also be used on walls.

Scribing
Trimming a moulding to fit another's profile where they intersect.

Scrim
Covering for joints where plasterboard is used to line walls: usually consists of hessian dipped in wet plaster. Scrim may also be used for covering ceiling joints when plasterboard is used.

Secret fixing
Fixings in joinery in which any screws used are hidden — often by overlapping an adjacent timber.

Section
Representation on a drawing of a building cut by an imaginery line to indicate its construction.

Septic tank
Tank in which waste is decomposed. Most septic tanks require emptying from time to time but in some cases waste may be dispersed through a soakaway.

Services
Gas, electricity, drainage and water provided to a house or block of flats.

Setting coat
In 3-coat plastering the final coat skimming the surface, smoothing it and ensuring that the work is in true plane.

Shackle
Method of securing joint betwen two timbers by means of a U-shaped metal fastening.

Shake
Crack in timber caused by weathering and the timber drying out rather than by fracture or damage through misuse or bad workmanship.

Shearing
Breaking apart of components when under excessive stress.

Shingle
Oak or Cedar used as a roofing tile available in different sizes.

Shoe
Fitted at the lower end of a down pipe to ensure that rain water coming down it discharges into gully.

Shooting
Dressing the edges of doors to ensure they fit the door frame accurately. Exterior doors may swell after prolonged wet weather; should this happen they may admit draughts if planed excessively when a spell of fine weather arrives.

Shore
A timber used as a prop to a building the upper end of which is fixed to a wall and the lower end of which is anchored into the ground. To spread the area of support given to the wall it is usual to line this with board where the upper end of the prop meets the wall so that the support offered is distributed over a greater area of the wall's surface.

Sill
Horizontal member at the foot of an opening such as a window. Window sills usually project out from the rest of the window frame to protect the wall immediately beneath them. Their upper surfaces are weathered (by sloping slightly downwards away from the house) to shed rain water and throated (grooved) beneath to prevent water seeping back to the wall and draining down it.

Skirting
Length of member (usually timber) along wall at its base to protect the wall's surface and cover joint between wall and floor.

Slate
Laminated rock capable of being split along parallel planes of cleverage into large flat sheets which, when trimmed to size, are used for roofing and dampcourses.

Sleeper wall
Low wall rising from ground level to provide support for a suspended floor constructed of joists and floorboards.

Slip joints
Unbonded joint (usually in brickwork) intended to permit slight movement.

Smoke shutters
Shutters of incombustible sheet material used under the lintel of a fireplace opening in an effort to prevent unsatisfactory flues emitting smoke into a room.

Sneck
Traditional type of lever for lifting a latch.

Soakers
Lead sheeting (or other suitable metal) used with flashing to render the junction between roof slates or tiles and the chimney stack or other vertical wall. Small soakers may also be used at window sills where they are slipped under the horn of the window.

Soffit
Underside. Term applies to virtually any architectural feature.

Softwood
Timber from coniferous trees.

Soil pipe
Pipe leading to foul drain from WCs. Usually fixed vertically.

Soldier course
Course of bricks set on end.

Sole plate
Timber bearing for a principal rafter.

Spall
Piece of stone knocked off a larger stone.

Spandrel
Triangular shaped area between the curves of a couple of adjacent arches and the horizontal moulding above them.

Spar
Hazel staple for securing thatch. Also a term formerly used for a rafter.

Spatter dash
Rendering for wall producing an uneven texture by flicking lumps of wet plaster at the wall being treated.

Splay
Slope or bevel above a door or window opening.

Springer
Where an arch starts to spring, i.e., where the curve starts to go inwards and upwards.

Sprocked piece
Short length of rafter secured to a common rafter at the latter's foot, to give part of the roof less slope so creating projecting eaves on a plane less steep than the roof proper.

Squinch
An arch across an interior angle.

Stanchion
Vertical support of steel or iron such as steel reinforcement in a concrete pillar or a vertical bar in iron work for an old window.

Steel trowel finish
Smooth finish to plaster or floor screen.

Stiles
Verticals in timber framing.

Stilted arch
Arch with its springing line higher than its impost.

Stock lock
Lock similar to rim lock but with a wooden casing.

Strap hinge
Hinge with a long plate fastened securely to a massive door.

Strapped
Battens secured to a wall for fixing laths.

Stretcher
Brick laid lengthways when building a wall.

Strings
Timber sides to staircase which supports the risers and treads.

Strip floors
Floor consisting of narrow floor boards which is less inclined to split or warp than floor with wider boards.

String course
Projecting band of masonry, brickwork or plaster around building usually at the same level as the first storey sills to provide decoration for the exterior of the building.

String course
Horizontal course of bricks or masonry projecting from a wall. Alternatively, a moulding projecting from a wall.

Strut
Short timbers connecting and supporting other structural timbers. Found mainly in older buildings.

Stuart
English architecture during period approximately from 1625 to just beyond 1700.

Stucco
Plaster work associated first with the Renaissance period. Became used for decoration on ceilings and walls and was popular at least up to the Victorian era and even into Edwardian times.

Stud
The smaller verticals in much timber frame construction. Studs were often used, more or less evenly spaced, in the walls. Studding is often found in partition walls.

Stylobate
Platform for a colonnade popular in classical architecture.

Summer
Term denoting beam to support floor joists in common use up to at least the end of the 17th Century when the term girder began to come into use.

Swag
Ornamental festoon taken up at the ends and dropping in the middle depicting fruit, foliage or flowers. Such garlands were usually moulded in plaster.

Swan neck
Short length of pipe used at the eaves gutter of a roof to bring the storm water back to the downpipe fixed close to the wall.

T

Tail
The part of a stone buried in a wall.

Tanking
Sealing a basement, usually with asphalt, to make it waterproof.

Template
A template (or templet) is a pattern usually cut from thin sheet material. May be used as a guide for a moulding or for cutting stone or other material.

Tenon
Formed at the end of a timber and cut to fit into a mortice.

Terrace
1. Row of houses joined together, the accommodation of each being separated by a party wall. 2. Raised ground around, or partly around, a house. 3, Lead covered flat room in the middle of some square buildings which requires adequate provision for draining stormwater.

Terracotta
Baked clay or earth used for such items as chimney pots. Usually harder than most bricks.

Terrazzo
Consisting of chippings of marble set in white or coloured cement. The surface is polished and is sometime used for stair treads as well as floors which need to be hard wearing.

Textured paints
Paint containing fine granular materials to produce textured finishes.

Three-coat plaster
Plaster laid in three coats. The first coat applied is usually the thickest and is the rendering coat which adhered to the base material and functions as a pricking up coat. The second coat is the floating coat and is keyed to receive the final coat which is usually the thin setting coat for producing the finished surface.

Throat
1. In a chimney just above the chimney back between the chimney opening and the flue proper. 2. Groove on the underside of a sill to throw off rain water and prevent it running down wall.

Through stones
Stones in a stone wall which either go right through its width or penetrate further into it than the majority of stones.

Thumb latch
Latch with a thumb piece for activating the sneck to go through the door lifting the latch on the other side. Also called a Norfolk latch.

Tie beam
A major roof truss is formed when a tie beam ties together the feet of the principal rafters. Such a tie beam runs from wall to wall tieing the wall plates together. Used in many mediaeval buildings.

Tile
Baked clay unit for covering roof or floor.

Tilting batten
Batten for tiling or slating positioned along the ridge of a roof.

Tilting fillet
Wedge-shaped batten running down the sides of valley gutters.

Tolerances
Acceptable dimensional differences in building and engineering units.

Tongue and groove boarding
One edge of such board has a projection which fits a slot on the other edge.

Toothing
Projecting bricks at the end of a wall to provide a bond should the wall be continued.

Torching
Mortar pointing sealing the heads of slates or tiles in a roof space.

Tracery
Patterned stonework in mediaeval window. Popular during Gothic period.

Transom
Horizontal stone or timber member dividing window openings into separate lights. A cross bar of a window. The flat stern of a houseboat.

Tread
Flat step in a staircase.

Trimmer
Floor joint fastening the sawn off ends of other joists where an opening occurs for, say a constructional fire hearth or staircase. Trimming joists are thicker than most joists as they support the ends of a trimmer joist.

Truss
Timber framework supporting longitudinal members of a roof.

Truss (Roof)
Strong framework of principal rafters.

Tudor
Phase of Elizabethan architecture in England.

Tuck pointing
Imitation pointing applied when joints have already been pointed up flush. The true pointing may need grooving out to accommodate the imitation pointing.

Tuscan
Roman Doric architecture is founded largely on the Tuscan order which originated in Tuscany.

U

Undercroft
The vaulted basement of a mediaeval building.

Universal beam
I-Section steel beam larger than an RSJ.

V

Valley
The re-entrant angle where two sloping roofs meet.

Vault
Chamber below ground level with a ceiling of arched stone or brick. Some vaulted roofs occur in chambers above ground level.

Venetian window
The Adam brothers made these arched openings with rectangular openings at the sides popular. The flat headed side openings are lower and narrower than the principal arched opening. Characteristic of the Palladian style of architecture.

Veranda
An open balcony, usually occurring on an upper storey.

Verges
Edge of a roof above a gable. Sometimes finished with barge boards.

Vermiculation
Stone or plaster decorated with worm-like intaglio ridges.

Vestibule
Anti chamber leading into a larger room.

Victorian
The architectural styles evolved from the middle of the 19th Century and the start of the 20th Century.

Villa
Originally a Roman residence of importance. Today a less significant semi detached house typical of the suburbs.

Volute
Spiral scroll forming part of the decoration of many Roman capitals.

Voussoir
Wedge shaped bricks or stones forming an arch.

W

Wagon
Semicircular roof in Romanesque style.

Wainscotting
Wall panelling.

Waling
Timber supporting the sides of a trench.

Wall plate
Timber running along top of wall to give bearing for rafters.

Wane
Timber with at least one edge showing the outside of the tree from which it was cut.

Waney edge
Weather boards with an irregular outline.

Water table
1 Level of saturated ground. 2. Slope in masonry such as where a buttress joins a wall's face.

Weatherstruck pointing
Pointing struck to throw water off wall face.

Web
Vertical part of an RSJ or steel beam linking the two horizontal flanges. The term is also sometimes used to denote filling a vault.

Whiting
Crushed chalk used as a filler or to make putty.

Winder
Steps in a staircase turning a corner without a half landing. The steps radiate from a centre and so are narrow on the inside and wide at the outside.

Wood float
Tool used in plastering.

Wreathed handrail
Handrail which curves at the lower newel in a decorative manner.

Wrought iron
Material used for shaping while hot from the forge.

This book is dedicated to all the architects, planners and other professionals whose work shapes our environment; to the builders and craftsmen erecting the fabric of our dwellings; to the manufacturers of building components; to the merchants who supply the builders' needs; to all the diy enthusiasts who lavish so much effort on repairing and maintaining their homes.

⏚ Building and Construction Books

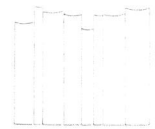

100 Avenue Road, London NW3 3TP Telephone: 01-935 6611. Telex 299973 ITP LN G Facsimile 01-586 5561

BUILDING TODAY

This is what you have been missing. The multi-useful **Building Today** every week. There's no other magazine like it in the United Kingdom.

Packed with current news, trade news, product news, features and jobs. **Building Today** caters especially for the needs of Britain's building industry, going behind the scenes with pages of insight into the people and events that make the news.

Current Prices — every week **Building Today** offers its readers the most up-to-date prices available for small quantities of materials collected from a builders' merchant. The Prices quoted are average and are compiled by computer from information supplied by merchants throughout the country immediately prior to publication. Readers should make adjustments to suit their particular conditions.

Estimating Guide — every month comprehensive up-dated estimating service, covering material, labour and plant prices (fourth week of month).

Monthly features — reviewing a wide range of subjects such as bricks, drainage, timber frame, housing and many more to provide the reader with factual details on new innovations and building systems as soon as they come onto the market.

These frequent collect-and-keep supplements on specialist topics are widely sought after.

Undoubtedly you can benefit professionally from **Building Today** by taking out a subscription.

Further details and a subscription form can be obtained by either ringing 01-935 6611 — Circulation Dept. — or writing to the Circulation Manager, BTJ, International Thomson Business Publishing, 100 Avenue Road, London NW3 3TP.

Building and Construction Books

100 Avenue Road, London NW3 3TP Telephone: 01-935 6611. Telex 299973 ITP LN G Facsimile 01-586 5561

Titles from Building & Construction Books

Arbitration for Contractors
Bonus — A Study of Incentive Schemes
Builder's Detail Sheets
Builder's Reference Book (12th Edition)
Building Regulations 1985 Explained (Revised Edition)
Buyer's Guide 1989
Cases in Construction Management
Construction Case Law in the Office
Contract Joinery
Designing and Submitting Plans for
    Single Storey House Extensions
Directory of Plant Hire
Directory of Sub-Contractors
Drainage Details
Estimating for Alterations and Repairs
Guide to Estimating Building Work 1988/89
Hot Water Details
Sanitation Details
Site Carpentry
Techniques of Routing
The Small Contractor's Guide to the Computer
UK Plant Market — 5 Year Review
Understanding JCT contracts
Practical Guide to Alterations and Improvements
Practical Guide to Basic Bookkeeping for Builders
Practical Guide to Blockwork
Practical Guide to Bookkeeping Principles Made Easy
Practical Guide to Builder's Questions and Answers
Practical Guide to Estimating Daywork Rates
Practical Guide to Groundworks & Foundations
Practical Guide to Rafter Calculations
Practical Guide to Repair and Maintenance of Houses
Practical Guide to Roofing
Practical Guide to Setting Out on Site
Practical Guide to Sub Contracting
Practical Guide to Windows

For further details on the above titles or for a booklet on prices etc. please ring Building & Construction Books department on 01-935 6611.